Bill Yenne

MALLARD
PRESS

First published in the United States of America in 1991
by The Mallard Press
Mallard Press and its accompanying design and logo are trademarks of BDD
Promotional Book Company, Inc.

Produced by Brompton Books Corp
15 Sherwood Place
Greenwich CT 06830

ISBN 0-7924-5547-9

Printed in Hong Kong

Below and opposite page: B movies were developed in response to the depression, and Republic Pictures became the king of B movie serials, making five Zorro serials between 1937 and 1947. George Turner starred as the son of Zorro in 1947. Clayton Moore, later the Lone Ranger, appeared as the ghost of Zorro in 1949, Republic's last Zorro serial.

Designed by Ruth DeJauregui
Captioned by Annie McGarry

GHOST OF ZORRO

featuring
CLAYTON MOORE · PAMELA BLAKE · ROY BARCROFT · GEORGE J. LEWIS

Written by
ROYAL COLE · WILLIAM LIVELY · SOL SHOR
Associate Producer FRANKLIN ADREON
Directed by FRED C. BRANNON
A REPUBLIC PICTURE

TERROR HAUNTS THE FAR FRONTIER!

Who rides behind the black mask of ZORRO!

59/203

CONTENTS

The Early Days

The Legend Begins

The legend of Zorro began — innocently enough — with the August 9, 1919 issue of the pulp magazine *All Story Weekly*. It was the first summer after the Great War, and the American public was in a good mood, ready for fun, ready for adventure.

It was a prosperous time for pulp magazines, such as *Argosy* (with which *All Story Weekly* would eventually merge), *Adventure* and *Western Story Weekly*. But *All Story Weekly* was the *crème de la crème*, the top of the heap, based largely on the success of Edgar Rice Burroughs' *Tarzan of the Apes*, which had been serialized in its pages since 1912.

Pulp magazines were a uniquely American creation. They took their name from the poor quality paper on which they were printed. Their covers were loud, garish and often racy. For a thin dime, you could follow a novel-sized story as it was serialized in the pulps from week to week. This serialization of stories became the forerunner of the cliffhanging films of the 1930s and 1940s, which in turn blazed the path for the concept of radio and television series. Frank Munsey had first launched the pulps when he took over the children's magazine *Argosy* and radically changed its format by exclusively publishing adult short stories. During their golden age, which ended with the Second World War, pulp magazines explored all the areas of popular literature: the police story (*Detective Story*, *Black Mask*), the Western (*Western Roundup*, *Western Story*), science fiction (*Amazing Stories*, *Astounding Stories*), horror (*Weird Tales*, *Horror Stories*) and romance (*Love Story*, *Husbands*). Pulp magazines came and went. They were too numerous to count, yet they published such

excellent authors as Edgar Rice Burroughs, Dashiell Hammett, Tennessee Williams, HP Lovecraft, and Ray Bradbury — at the standard rate of a penny a word — as they created such immortal heroes as Tarzan, Sam Spade, and Hopalong Cassidy.

Enter one Johnston McCulley, a 36-year-old former police reporter who had served as an Army public affairs officer during the First World War and was now ready to try his hand at pulp fiction. This is not to say that police reporting in the early days of this century did not impinge upon the domain of the fictional. Indeed, it was characterized by the fast, hot sensationalism that made the *Police Gazette* one of America's leading tabloids. McCulley, who was born on February 2, 1883 in Ottawa, Illinois, had been on the tabloid beat for most of his adult life. He had published his first adventure novel, *The Lord of Lost Hope*, in 1908. Soon after he moved to Southern California.

His story, *The Curse of Capistrano*, is set in early nineteenth century California — the 'days of the dons' — at a time when Los Angeles was still part of Spanish-controlled Mexico. It tells the saga of Don Diego de la Vega, the son of a rich Californian family. His outward demeanor is that of an idle youth who prefers poetry to violent competition. But when night comes, he transforms himself into Zorro ('fox' in Spanish), who combats the local authorities and delivers people from the yoke of oppression. McCulley had no intention of making Zorro his life's work, but

Above: A sleepy Southern California hacienda was a typical Zorro setting. *Opposite page:* On the second 'Zoro' cover, our hero's image is unlike what we've come to expect. No copies are known to exist of McCulley's first *Curse of Capistrano* installment. The promised movie starring Douglas Fairbanks was never produced.

ARGOSY
ALL-STORY
WEEKLY

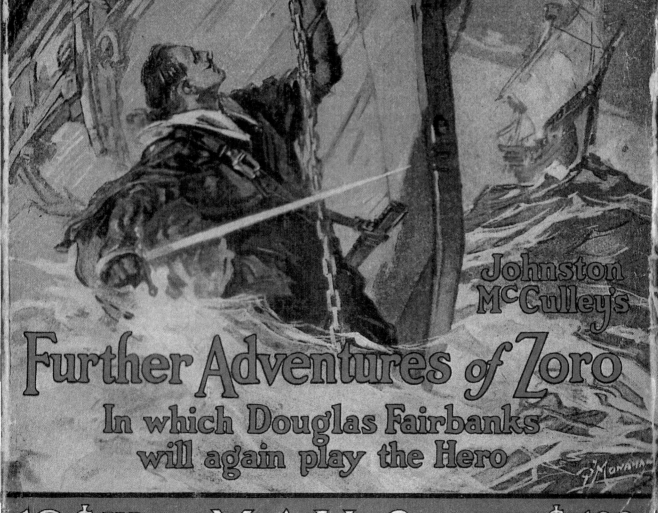

Johnston
McCulley's

Further Adventures of Zoro

In which Douglas Fairbanks
will again play the Hero

10 ¢ PER COPY   MAY 6   BY THE YEAR $4.00

after a few installments of *The Curse of Capistrano* were devoured by the public, it became clear that *All Story* and Johnston McCulley had a hit on their hands which was bigger than anyone could have imagined.

As he first appeared in 1919, McCulley's new character embodied the time-tested theme of the righter of wrongs, the defender of the weak and oppressed. One might compare Zorro to Robin Hood, but the closest model would probably have to be the Scarlet Pimpernel, conceived in 1905 by the Hungarian-born English novelist Baroness Emmuska Orczy. In her series of novels, which were very much in vogue in English-speaking countries, Orczy introduced a character endowed with a double identity. By day, he was Sir Percy Blackeney, an effete and cowardly English country squire, who, when the circumstances required, revealed himself to be the Scarlet Pimpernel, a swashbuckler and the valiant champion of the French aristocracy.

Zorro's World

To understand Zorro as a character, it is necessary to first understand a little about the historical setting in which Johnston McCulley placed him. Like Robin Hood's Sherwood Forest, the Southern California of the 1830s was well outside of the mainstream of the events of world history. An amateur historian who had by now lived in California for several years, McCulley knew some essential historical facts about the area and used these as his canvas.

However, McCulley either knew very little about the precise details of California history or cared very little about them. As a result, it is almost impossible to date Zorro exactly, and McCulley himself never gives the reader a date. For example, McCulley definitely refers to a time when Spain still controlled California. Don Diego was, after all, a young Spanish caballero. When one takes into account the reliance on swords rather than on guns, and that what guns existed were muskets, one is led to the impression that McCulley meant the 1820s. However, in actual California history, this was an era of the missions. There were no great haciendas for a Spanish dandy like Diego to inhabit. McCulley just jumbled California history together in a fashion

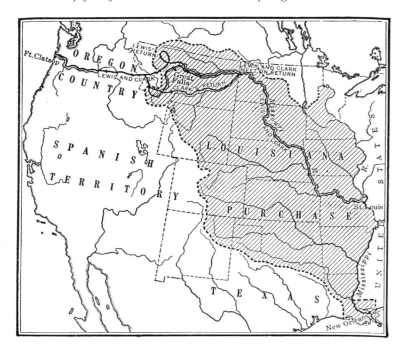

Above: Spain once controlled much more of North America than Mexico and California. *Right:* McCulley creatively interpreted California history, combining elements of the eras of both the haciendas and the missions under Spanish control.

Above: McCulley may have drawn inspiration from a number of California legends, including contemporaries of the infamous bandito Joaquin Murieta (1830-1853). Romantic legend has flourished around this miner who struck back at the gold-seeking gringos who overran the Mexican settlement of San Andreas. At least 13 murders were attributed to Murieta and his gang before Captain Harry Love allegedly killed him. *Below:* There was some dispute as to whether or not the head actually belonged to Joaquin, who was seen as an advocate for the oppressed Mexicans. *Opposite:* Frank Munsey's transformation of *Argosy* into an adult magazine launched the pulp phenomenon.

WILL BE EXHIBITED

FOR ONE DAY ONLY!

AT THE STOCKTON HOUSE!

THIS DAY, AUG. 12, FROM 9 A. M., UNTIL 6, P. M.

THE HEAD

Of the renowned Bandit!

JOAQUIN!

AND THE

HAND OF THREE FINGERED JACK!

THE NOTORIOUS ROBBER AND MURDERER.

that can never be adequately sorted out. For example, some action takes place in the 'presidio' of Los Angeles, even though the only presidios in California were located in San Francisco and Monterey. McCulley entitles his first work, *The Curse of Capistrano*, even though the entire story takes place a hundred miles north in Los Angeles. Inconsistencies pile up on top of inconsistencies. Fortunately, McCulley's writings are a good read, so if you ever happen to pick up some original Zorro stories, just sit back, relax and abandon all literary criticism.

Mexico was born as New Spain in 1522, and by the seventeenth century the colony had been expanded to include what is now the state of California. Mexico became independent of the Spanish empire in 1822.

California remained part of Mexico until achieving some measure of autonomy in 1838. The United States defeated Mexico in the Mexican War of 1846-1848 and by February 2, 1848, Mexico surrendered its remaining claims to California. In the meantime, in 1845, the ethnic American majority in northern California had staged a revolution which had brought independence to California. After 1848, steps were taken that led to the California Republic becoming a state in 1850.

Though ultimately destined to become home to eight million people, California's largest city, Los Angeles, in 1919, had a population of less than 100,000 and was still a sleepy village of little importance in any grand scheme. While San Francisco eventually evolved into the state's cosmopolitan metropolis, Los Angeles continued to be deeply rooted in its Hispano-Mexican heritage.

Los Angeles itself had been founded on September 4, 1781 when Governor Felipe de Neve, a representative of King Ferdinand VII of Spain, created the village as El Pueblo de Nuestra Senora la Reyna de Los Angeles de Rio Porciunculo. Located midway on a two-day ride between the forts at Santa Barbara and San Diego, Los Angeles was intended to function as a purely agricultural outpost to insure the food supply of the larger posts. The colonists—46 people from 11 families—laid out a city. By 1821, when Zorro might have been on the scene, Los Angeles had a population of 700.

In December 1831, a company of 30 men, under the command of Lieutenant Colonel Don Manuel Victoria, Mexico's chief of military operations for California, rode into the pueblo of Los Angeles. Authoritarian and arrogant, Victoria had as his goal the suppression of California's political secularization, which had taken shape under his predecessor. Furious at seeing California falling back under the religious and political control of Imperial Mexico, many people revolted, and in Los Angeles, an outnumbered army of 200 conspirators assembled to fight Victoria's soldiers. Among them was José Maria Avila, a man well known for his courage and horsemanship.

Early in the ensuing battle, Avila identified Victoria and engaged him in a fierce one-on-one duel. Gravely injured, Victoria withdrew to the Mission San Gabriel before being evacuated back to Mexico. José Maria Avila entered the realm of legend, and McCulley later may have drawn upon some of his exploits in the creation of Zorro.

There may have been a basis for an historical Zorro beyond the legend of José Maria Avila. Salomon Maria Simeon Pico was born near Salinas, California on September 5, 1821. He lived in the Monterey Bay area until 1844 when he moved to the Sierra Nevada foothill country of today's Tuolumne and Stanislaus counties, where his legend became intertwined with that of California's most notorious nineteenth century outlaw, Joaquin Murieta (1830-1853).

Pico found himself on the wrong side of California's War of Independence and thereafter swore vengeance upon the Ameri-

Above: General Andres Pico and his brother Pio *(below)* were politically prominent cattle ranchers who owned about 10,000 acres (including 35 miles of coastline) in San Diego in the early 1800's. Andres led Californios against US troops at the Battle of San Pasqual and signed the Capitulation of Cahuenga treaty which closed the Mexican War in California. Pio Pico was the last Mexican governor of California. *At right:* The mission San Gabriel is famous for its wall of bells *(below, right)* which was destroyed in the 1812 earthquake, and later rebuilt. *The Curse of Capistrano* was not actually set in this mission. *Opposite page:* A statue of a saint from the mission at San Juan Capistrano.

cans. In 1849, with the Gold Rush underway and California statehood just around the corner, Pico drifted south to the Santa Barbara area where he became a highwayman. With his take often running as high as $150,000 in gringo gold, Pico earned a reputation that fluctuated between that of a Robin Hood and a ghoul, depending on whether it was a Californio or an American doing the describing. It might be added that he had the nasty habit of stringing the ears of his victims on a rawhide thong!

In November 1851, he rode into Los Angeles to attempt the defense of two brothers he perceived as having been wrongly accused of murder. In the resulting shoot-out, United States Judge Benjamin Hayes found himself with a bullet hole through his hat courtesy of Pico, who quickly vanished into the night.

In 1857 Pico moved to Baja California, which was and still is part of Mexico, to take a job as Captain of the Guard for Baja Governor Jose Castro, but in April 1860 Castro was assassinated. What followed was a situation that can be said to have been analogous to the 1990s extradition by Colombia of Medelin drug kings to the United States. Castro's successor had decided to get tough with all the Californios and Mexicans living in Baja who were wanted by law enforcement officials in the United States.

Justice was swift. On May 1, 1860, Pico and several companions were arrested at a dance party, marched outside and shot.

Historian Marilyn Ailes, the world's foremost expert on Pico's life, believes that the 1851 Los Angeles incident was probably McCulley's inspiration and that the legend of that night is in fact

pure Zorro. According to Ailes, McCulley moved the legend back two decades so that Zorro's antagonists would be the aloof Imperial aristocracy rather than post-1850 Americans. However, as even she points out, 'Zorro is much more than Salomon Pico.'

Indeed he is.

In summary, Zorro may well have been an amalgam of Pico, Murieta and Avila, combined with a dose of the Scarlet Pimpernel, and all fired by a generous helping of McCulley's own imagination.

From the tile roofs to the adobe-walled courtyards, the architecture of southern California had changed little in the century that separated McCulley from the era of his masked avenger. Place names were still the same, and it was easy for Johnston McCulley to step out on his veranda on a warm spring night and imagine what it would have been like there in Zorro's time.

As we've noted, McCulley used Los Angeles for the mood rather than the historic fact. He took license with reality as he smelled the eucalyptus groves planted in the late nineteenth century and grafted them into the landscape of Zorro's world. He also constructed an imaginary California in which mission and hacienda life coexisted as they never did in historic reality. However, few would pick at such nits. McCulley's California bore the same relationship to the real Spanish California that New York City did to the Gotham City which Bob Kane would create for Batman. Indeed, it is interesting to note that at the height of Batmania following the release of the *Batman* movie in 1989, Kane freely admitted in his autobiography that *Zorro* had been the original inspiration for *his* character.

Think for a moment about what Bob Kane did. He simply took one black cloaked creature of the night, the fox, and changed him into another, the bat. He retained an effete filthy rich alter ego, calling his Don Diego, Bruce Wayne. Both Batman and Zorro would enter their secret cave at night. While Zorro would sally forth on his black stallion, Toronado, Batman would leave his cave by another form of horsepower, a black Batmobile.

Both Zorro and Batman have manservant accomplices. Both prefer non-ballistic weaponry. Kane's particular genius was in simply taking Zorro and putting him in modern Manhattan instead of Alta California. While addressing this issue head on, Batman is hardly the only Zorro imitator to make it big. Other examples include Superman, The Lone Ranger, and, more recently, four masked swordsmen who live in a sewer instead of a cave and who are green instead of black. These are, of course, the Teenage Mutant Ninja Turtles.

As for McCulley's California, the mood was there. All that was missing was the myth, and McCulley soon supplied that.

The Curse of Capistrano

McCulley's first Zorro story was entitled *The Curse of Capistrano*. This is peculiar since the story takes place in Los Angeles. The mission of San Juan Capistrano (the place to which the swallows return each year) is actually about one day's ride by horse *south* of Los Angeles at the juncture of today's US Highway 101 and Interstate 5. In the story, Capistrano is nowhere to be seen.

Having constructed his secret alter ego a decade before at age 15, McCulley's Zorro began employing his skills at age 25. As he explains it, 'The time came and my work began.'

His work is that of the legend of Avila and Pico, a Robin Hood career of defending the rights of the downtrodden and rectifying injustice with the slash of a cold, steel blade.

McCulley gave little thought to Zorro's future life when he wrote that first story, as he intended for Zorro to retire after *Capistrano*. Indeed, Zorro even unmasks himself at the story's conclusion. However, this fact was conveniently forgotten when Zorro's popularity surged. Upon his return opposite Don Diego in *The Further Adventures of Zorro*, McCulley places him back in costume, while all the surrounding characters simply forget that they have seen Zorro take off his mask at the end of *Capistrano*.

Below: The Mission of San Juan Capistrano was built in 1776 by the Franciscans in order to instruct the Indians in Christian teachings and 'civilized' ways. The missionaries discouraged their tribal customs, and taught them to cultivate the land and construct mission buildings. McCulley probably used Capistrano in his title for its alliterative quality. *Opposite:* Capistrano's mission fountain.

Hollywood Discovers Zorro

Los Angeles may have been a sleepy provincial settlement when McCulley penned *The Curse of Capistrano*, but that fact would soon change. The movies were coming to town.

During the second half of the nineteenth century, due to the construction of a succession of transcontinental rail lines, Los Angeles had grown and expanded. In the 1880s, Harvey Henderson Wilcox, a real estate broker, settled in Cahuenga Valley, where he bought up vast tracts of land that he then carved into lots. He called his new town Hollywood.

For the most part, early American film companies had settled in New York, New Jersey, or Illinois—where the people were. However, the fledgling filmmakers found themselves confronted with endless problems, including unpredictable weather. A gentle snowfall might occur in the middle of shooting a scene meant to take place in the Sahara Desert! The transformation of Hollywood from a quiet subdivision began with Colonel William Selig, president of the Selig Polyscope Company, who decided to send a film company to southern California to take advantage of the area's sun and stable climate.

In 1909, one of Selig's directors, Francis Boggs, rented a former Chinese laundry at the corner of 8th and Olive Streets, where he installed offices and dressing rooms. In the neighboring lot, he built an 1100-square-foot stage for the production of *The Heart of a Race Trout*, the first film produced entirely in California.

They soon discovered that Hollywood provided much more than sun. Extras and labor were abundant and inexpensive, while the surrounding open country offered a profusion of varied natural settings that could, depending on their needs, evoke the Wild West, the mysterious Orient or ancient Egypt. In the outlying ranches, it was possible to rent all the horses necessary for the Westerns. What's more, it never snowed on any Sahara Desert constructed in Hollywood.

Soon this small corner of Los Angeles became a household word, and the name that was to be most often associated with that household word was Douglas Fairbanks.

Below: Zorro's popularity could not be 'fenced' in. He leapt from the pulpy pages of *Argosy*, where the stories were first printed, to the silver screen (*opposite page*) in the person of Douglas Fairbanks, the first actor to portray Zorro.

Deftly Zorro flipped the blade from the capitán's fist

Zorro Rides Again

DOUGLAS FAIRBANKS

IN

'THE MARK OF ZORRO'

DIRECTED BY FRED NIBLO

FROM THE "ALL STORY WEEKLY" NOVEL
"THE CURSE OF CAPISTRANO"
BY JOHNSTON McCULLEY

Born Douglas Elton Ulman in Denver on May 2, 1883, the same year that marked the birth of Johnston McCulley, Fairbanks had embarked on a successful stage career at 18. He turned to the silent screen in 1915. Lured to Hollywood by a generous contract with Triangle Films, Fairbanks starred in 26 silent films between 1915 and 1918, including *The Mystery of the Leaping Fish*, *The Matrimaniac*, *The Americano* and *A Modern Musketeer*. Indeed, it was the latter film, released in 1918, that paved the way for Zorro. Eleven of these first 26 films were produced by Fairbanks himself, and many of them were directed by the legendary David Mark 'DW' Griffith.

A small, but athletic man, Fairbanks evolved from 1915 to 1934 into one of Hollywood's most memorable heroes. He was D'Artagnan, Robin Hood, Don Juan, Robinson Crusoe, the Thief of Baghdad, and he gave life to Zorro. He thus established himself as the reigning king of adventure films. Fairbanks was also an excellent comedian, and knew how to move beyond his star status by becoming involved in film production. In 1919, he founded United Artists, in association with Charlie Chaplin, DW Griffith, and Mary Pickford, with whom he'd fallen in love during a war bond promotion tour in 1918. Known as 'America's Sweetheart,' Pickford became Doug's sweetheart. He divorced Anna Beth Sully—the mother of Douglas Fairbanks, Jr—to marry her.

In 1920, in the first of Hollywood's great 'royal' weddings, Douglas Fairbanks married the movie capital's favorite leading lady and 'America's Sweetheart,' Mary Pickford. It was during their honeymoon in Europe that Fairbanks happened to pick up one of the issues of *All Story Weekly* that he'd tossed in his steamer trunk at the behest of theatrical agent Ruth Allen. It was the August 9, 1919 number with *The Curse of Capistrano*. The story fell on the King of Hollywood like a ton of bricks. No sooner did he and his new bride return to their imposing Pickfair estate in Beverly Hills than he set to work—under the pseudonym Elton Thomas—to turn McCulley's story into the screenplay which

Right: Douglas Fairbanks, Sr as the swashbuckling hero and Marguerite de la Motte as Lolita in a particularly melodramatic moment from *The Mark of Zorro*. The costumes here seem more realistic than the poses. Compare the Hollywood wardrobe to a 19th century engraving *(above)* of a Spanish member of the Alta California population.

would be produced by United Artists as *The Mark of Zorro*.

With the able Fred Niblo in the director's chair and Fairbanks himself as producer, the filming was underway in a matter of weeks. It was a low-budget film, but then there really hadn't yet been any multimillion dollar epics by that time. Fairbanks cast Marguerite de la Motte as Lolita, Robert McKim as the evil Captain Ramon and Noah Beery as Sergeant Gonzales. For the Zorro/Don Diego part he, of course, cast himself.

Released in November 1920, *The Mark of Zorro* was just the escape that audiences were hungry for with something for everyone—romance, heroism, adventure—and was very well received for its era. Fairbanks himself is fantastic, alternating between the exaggerated languor of the pathetic Don Diego with his parasol ('I detest swords and bloodshed'), to the athletic and virile Zorro.

All of the essential ingredients for a great adventure are present. Fairbanks as the fiery Zorro is full of panache and graceful elegance, his face endowed with a sparkling smile but masked by a black velvet half mask. There are two well-choreographed sword fights between Fairbanks and McKim that climax with the signature 'Z' being slashed into the flesh of the villain's neck. This effect, created by Fairbanks, was so powerful that McCulley borrowed it for his own future tellings of the Zorro legend. In later stories the 'Z' would no longer be cut into flesh but rather into clothing and wooden fixtures. In 1920, however, Zorro's modus was still just a notch away from Pico's rawhide thong of human ears.

This film was intended, of course, as a showcase for its producer and star, but in retrospect, it is now also seen as a showcase for its mythical hero. Indeed, it is Zorro who had all the best lines—or in the case of this silent film, the best subtitles.

'Justice for all! Punishment for the oppressors of the helpless!' Zorro declares with proletarian fervor, turning to Lolita to add, 'I'd make the desert a million roses yield—to die in shame before your beauty.'

What more could a lady want, except perhaps to know the true identity of her mysterious suitor?

The definitive line is pulled directly from the legend—if not the actual words—of Pico and Avila. Zorro announces that 'The heaven-kissed hills of your native California swarm with the sentinels of oppression. Our country's out of joint. It is for us caballeros and us alone to set it right. Justice for all!'

The Mark of Zorro ends happily, as justice is established, Zorro reveals himself to Lolita and happiness descends upon those heaven-kissed hills.

Fade to black.

For Douglas Fairbanks, it would be five years before he would again fade to the black of Zorro's cape and mask, but in the meantime, he was not far out of character. In a sense, *The Mark of Zorro* created Douglas Fairbanks as much as Douglas Fairbanks created Zorro. Both existed prior to 1920, of course, but both were more clearly defined as archetypes by their collaboration.

Fairbanks followed this immense box office success with similar roles in *The Three Musketeers* (1921), *Robin Hood* (1922) and *The Thief of Baghdad* (1924). Finally, in 1925, Fairbanks returned—figuratively—to the heaven-kissed hills of Southern California for the long-awaited sequel.

This time the story was inspired not by Johnston McCulley but by *Don Q's Love Story*, a novel by Kate and Hesketh Pritchard. The novel's action unfolded at the court of the Queen of Spain, where the young Don Cesar de Vega has been sent by his father, Don Diego—alias Zorro—to finish his education. When Cesar is accused wrongly of the murder of the Archduke of Austria, Zorro arrives on the scene to uncover the guilty party. Having benefited from his earlier swashbuckler films, in *Don Q, the Son of Zorro*

Opposite page: The cover to a press kit distributed to theaters before the local premier. *At top:* The friendly Don Q, pictured here with bullwhip, and Don Q *(above)* in a more pensive mood. These ad slicks were distributed for newspaper columns. *Overleaf:* The press kit's ads and suggestions for merchandise tie-ins.

DOUGLAS FAIRBANKS

"DON Q SON OF ZORRO"

Exhibitors Campaign Book

This book outlines publicity, advertising and exploitation matter that will enable any exhibitor, in any sized city, to put this Douglas Fairbanks feature over to big box-office results. There are many newspaper stories, one, two and three column advertising cuts, one, two and three column scene cuts for newspaper use, reproductions of the lithograph posters, the lobby display cards and slides, and the music cue sheet.

Two Column Advertising Cuts That Stand Out and Attract

XXD-3—Two Column Advertising Cut. Price 50 cents. Mats 10 cents.

Merchandise Tie-Ups

Harness shops are a curiosity now. Frame it up with the proprietor of one to advertise the showing of the "Don Q" whip on a side street where you will now find the harness-maker, who formerly occupied palatial quarters on the main drag. Let him claim that he has the only whips like those used in the picture. That gives a human interest tie-up, as well. Interviews with the harness-maker on the making and use of these whips offer another chance to get your picture into the papers.

FLORISTS—Doug meets his lady love in a garden, full of potted plants, etc. Chance here for tie-ups with florists.

FURNITURE—Doug's bed required a step ladder to get into. If big furniture dealers in the city can match this bed, or come anywhere near it, it will make a great stunt for the picture, carrying stills showing the bed, Doug, et al.

Trigger Action
And startling surprises feature this great Fairbanks picture. The finest adventure tale ever screened. The dashing, daring, Don Q bars all worry and you live in laughs and thrills.
Fast as Lightning

XXD-4—Two Column Advertising Cut. Price 50 cents. Mats 10 cents.

Advertising Cuts That Will Pull For the Box-Office

DOUGLAS FAIRBANKS in "DON Q, SON OF ZORRO"

XX-5—*Three Column Scene Cut (coarse) for Newspaper Use. Price 75 cents. Mats 20 cents.*

With a whip for a weapon Douglas Fairbanks gives more laughs, more real thrills, more high speed, in "Don Q" than in any picture he has ever made.

DOUGLAS FAIRBANKS

"DON Q SON OF ZORRO"

XXD-1—*One Column Advertising Cut Price 30 cents. Mats 5 cents.*

Three views of Douglas Fairbanks as "Don Q, Son of Zorro," and one of Zorro himself, also portrayed by the versatile Fairbanks in his latest screen feature. "Don Q" had its New York premiere at the Globe Theatre, and was generally acclaimed as one of the best films Fairbanks ever produced. It is an adventure-romance, frankly a melodrama, and filled with swift action and humor and in it the star does more stunts than in any other production he ever offered.—F

Special Publicity Cut—Three Column (coarse) for Newspaper Use.
Price 75 cents. Mats 20 cents. Order by Letter F.

Fairbanks attains a sort of perfection by playing both roles—father and son. The film was directed by the actor Donald Crisp, who also played the villain, Don Sebastian.

Don Q, the Son of Zorro found the aging swashbuckler in his forties (both Fairbanks and McCulley were now 42). Perhaps it was Fairbanks' own mid-life crisis that found him deciding to play both father and son in the film. Nevertheless, the rigors of the dual role found the venerable Doug's skill with blade and bull-whip undiminished. Meanwhile, young Cesar proved himself to be a chip off the Fox's block. In this sequel, it is Cesar who is positioned romantically opposite the love interest, the beautiful Doña Dolores, so aptly portrayed by Mary Astor. In the true spirit of high melodrama, we first meet Doña Dolores as Cesar approaches her in her garden with a rose in his hand. Under the direction of Donald Crisp, the plot thickens as Archduke Paul (Warner Oland) is murdered by the wicked Don Sebastian, who is played by Crisp himself. Cesar is blamed, feigns suicide and secretly summons his father from Mexico. Together the two de la Vegas clear the family name. Cesar and Doña Dolores then live happily ever after.

Crisp and Fairbanks planned to make *Don Q* a 'bigger' film than its predecessor in terms of the number and nature of sword-fights, dramatic escapes and intricacies of plot. The setting, too, is grander. Southern California, as we've noted, was a colonial backwater, with modest architecture, while Spain was a wonderland filled with castles that had great halls, dungeons and lush furnishings.

Like *The Mark of Zorro*, *Don Q* was a box office success and an excellent showcase for Fairbanks' talents. Despite their success, both films were silent. Zorro didn't speak. It would be another ten years before the American Pimpernel was to be endowed with the power of speech—but it would not be Fairbanks'. Although Zorro as a character is overshadowed by Don Cesar, his presence is maintained throughout the film. The younger de la Vega constantly alludes to his father, which paints Zorro in larger-than-life hues. When Don Cesar is asked where he learned to use the whip, he responds: 'In California. My father taught me. My father is the greatest man in America.' Later, as Don Cesar duels with Don Sebastian, the former remarks, 'You know, my father is the greatest swordsman in America.'

More significant, however, is the moral framework superimposed on Don Cesar by his father: 'My father always said,' he tells Don Sebastian, 'when you are in the right, fight; when you are in the wrong, acknowledge it.'

The Further Adventures of Johnston McCulley

Surprised as much as he was thrilled by the box office triumph of his character, Johnston McCulley had brought Zorro back to life in a six-part, 31-chapter series in *All Story Weekly*, which began on May 6, 1922. This series, which was given the obvious, if unimaginative, title *The Further Adventures of Zorro*, found McCulley to be strongly influenced by Douglas Fairbanks' adaptation of Zorro. For example, McCulley's original Don Diego was not nearly so exaggerated in his foppishness, but having seen him this way in *The Mark of Zorro*, McCulley gladly recast him as little more than a pathetic sissy. McCulley also borrowed Fairbanks' idea of having Diego perform silly napkin tricks at inopportune moments.

Although Grosset & Dunlap issued *The Curse of Capistrano* in book form under the title *The Mark of Zorro* in 1924, it was not until 1931—two years into the Great Depression—that McCulley decided to resume the stories featuring the character that had become his trademark. The title of his new series foreshadowed what was to come, as *All Story Weekly* brought out the first of four installments of *Zorro Rides Again* on October 3, 1931. For the next three years, McCulley annually gave *All Story Weekly* one single-issue installment of the adventures of his masked hero. However, it would not be until the 1940s that McCulley would pen the great majority of his Zorro stories.

By the mid-1930s, however, Zorro had a serious cult following and Johnston McCulley had become a celebrity. There was much cross-fertilization between the pulp fiction world and the film industry. McCulley inspired Fairbanks, and Fairbanks in turn influenced McCulley. In 1936, McCulley was summoned to Hollywood to write screenplays and provide fresh material for the newly formed Republic Pictures. *The Bold Caballero* was to be their first major film, and Republic didn't skimp on costs. Trucolor made its Republic debut, and also for the first time, Zorro

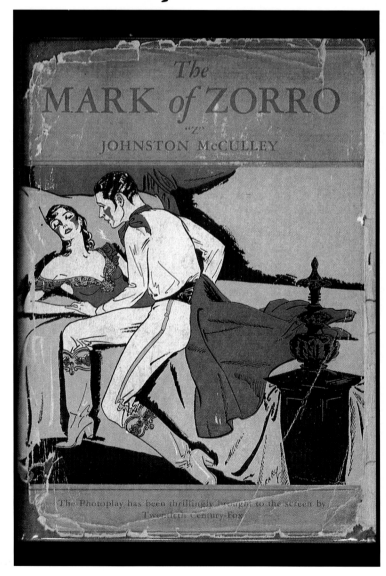

Right: The Curse of Capistrano was re-released in book form under the title of *The Mark of Zorro* in 1924. *Opposite page:* Mary Astor appeared as the beautiful Doña Dolores, the love interest of Don Cesar, played by Fairbanks.

Cordially,
Mary Astor

The courier galloped full tilt into the sleepy street, scattering the natives like paper in the wind

Black Grandee

By JOHNSTON McCULLEY
Author of "Senor Vulture," "The Tainted Caballero," etc.

Down the King's High Road he came, swift and unsuspected as the evil he would do, bearing the warrant of the Crown for the vengeance that spurred him on. An exciting novel of Old California

spoke, with Robert Livingstone adding the American Pimpernel's voice in the title role.

On the heels of the success of *The Bold Caballero*, Republic produced, and Fred Kohler directed, *The Vigilantes Are Coming*, in which an ersatz Zorro, portrayed by Robert Livingstone, is a young rancher determined to avenge the death of his father in the disguise of 'The Eagle.' For this and later serials, Livingstone learned fencing from Fred Cravens, the same master who had taught Douglas Fairbanks and Tyrone Power their moves with the blade.

In the meantime, Johnston McCulley's own career was becoming multifaceted. It was during this time that McCulley wrote several of his most memorable non-Zorro novels, including *The Black Star* (1921), *The Demon* (1925) and *The Rollicking Rogue* (1939). He also wrote a number of pulp stories under such *noms de plume* as Raley Brien, George Drayne, Frederic Phelps and Rowena Raley. However, he continued to be most well-known for

his Zorro character, and he must have realized that no matter what else he did with his life, his epitaph would read, 'Here lies the man who gave the world Zorro.'

Nonetheless, having created one winning character, McCulley was anxious for new writing challenges, longing—in vain, as it turned out—to generate other spectacular successes. The magic had worked once with Zorro and he hoped it would work again. It didn't, but he was still able to earn a very comfortable living. McCulley went on to create other heroes who would appear again and again, such as The Black Star, The Spider, The Avenging Twins and The Thunderbolt, but these never earned him the success that Zorro had—and would. McCulley continued his prolific output. Meanwhile, he created a number of 'surrogate Zorros' that included a Don Renegade, the rider from the pampas, Señor Devil-May-Care, Señor Vulture, Don Peon and the mercurial Black Grandee, but the success of these protagonists never came even remotely close to that of Zorro.

Don Peon

A Novel of Spanish California

By JOHNSTON McCULLEY
Author of the "Zorro" stories, etc.

"LET'S HAVE HIS HEART FOR BREAKFAST!"
BARTOLO'S BROTHER CRIED

The gay laughter of wealthy dons and lovely señoritas! The rebel cry of peons degraded beyond their endurance! And one man, the proudest of them all, fated to be treated lower than his own slave!

McCulley, anxious for writing challenges and success apart from his most popular creation, even tried writing pulp fiction under pseudonyms. He created a whole gallery of other heroes, including a number of pseudo-Zorros, the Black Grandee and Don Peon among them. None came close to the enormous success of Zorro. On the title page (*opposite page*), aside from the author's own famous name, no overt reference to Zorro is made, whereas Don Peon's literary cousin is mentioned *above*.

Action · Thrills · Adventure

ARGOSY

10¢

AUG. 22

WEEKLY

Don Peon
A New Novel of Romance
and High Adventure in
Zorro-Land by

Johnston McCulley

Theodore Roscoe
Cornell Woolrich
Donald Barr Chidsey
Allan Vaughan Elston

Don Peon (*above*) and Don Renegade (*opposite page*) were two of the many heroes that McCulley created while enjoying his immense success with Zorro. Here they are as they appeared on the cover of *Argosy* magazine. McCulley enjoyed a great demand for his stories.

Opposite page: Don Renegade, the 'rider from the pampas', and Don Peon had much in common with McCulley's most famous creation. Exciting romance and high adventure, action, fire and fury, sabers, dons, and a thrill-a-minute, all in 'Zorro-land' — Spanish California.

A Thrill-a-Minute *SAVOY* and *FISHER* *Novelet*
By **DONALD BARR CHIDSEY**

ARGOSY

WEEKLY

All the fire and fury
of exciting romance
in Old California

JOHNSTON McCULLEY'S
SUPERB NEW NOVEL

Don Renegade

The Republic Serials

The Depression had hit American cinema hard at the beginning of the 1930s, and the number of movie goers dropped to an all-time low. For the most part, the big film companies owned their own circuit of movie theaters, and they decided to react to this marketing dilemma by offering *two* films—an A and a B—instead of just one film per showing. Thus the 'B movie' was born. Movies released as such were bonuses. When the studio produced them, however, it was under the caveat that the costs be kept as low as possible. Because in those days actors were under contract to studios, the B departments of the major studios, such as Paramount, Fox, Warners, MGM, and Columbia, could use the best actors and directors under contract. While the B movies represented only a small portion of the activity of the big studios, they frequently constituted the fundamental production of smaller studios like Eagle, PRC, Monogram or Republic, the last of which eventually became the most famous of the B production companies.

Consisting of 20-minute episodes, B-movie 'serials' were the kind of films that adventure film lovers could catch each week in their favorite movie theaters. In this sense, they were a true precursor of the half-hour adventure dramas that were to become the staple of American television in the 1950s and 1960s. Between 1929 and 1956, Hollywood produced some 230 serials featuring Zorro, Flash Gordon, Superman, Batman, Dick Tracy, and many others that were inspired by popular novels and comic strips. After World War II, however, prosperity returned and the serials began to disappear.

The cover *(above, right)* and scenes from the serial pictorial featuring Reed Hadley as Zorro, and *(opposite page)* William Corson, Hadley and Sheila Darcy; *(above)* Hadley, Paul Marian and Don Del Oro; *(below)* Guy D'Ennery, Hadley and Corson.

By this time, the legend of Zorro was well established, but it is amazing how varied the views of the American Pimpernel were to become after only *three* films. Republic now moved to exploit the success of their 1936 Zorro feature film with the first of five 12-part serials. The public had already met Zorro, the son of Zorro and a Zorro imitator, so Republic decided to base the first serial on a story featuring Zorro's *grandson* in *Zorro Rides Again*. Set in then-contemporary (1937) California, this Zorro tale centered upon James Vega, portrayed by John Carroll, who was presumably Don Cesar's *son* (although that would seem to stretch the timeline a bit). Zorro indeed rides again—but this time in automobiles and airplanes!

Instead of his signature blade, this 'Zorro' brandished two revolvers and a long bullwhip. At one point, when his foot is pinched in the switch of a railroad track, and at another, when he loses his balance at the top of a Manhattan skyscraper, Young Vega saves himself by using his trusty whip. Carroll, who was content to play the effete James Vega and to break into an occasional song, was replaced in every action scene by the immortal stuntman Yakima Canutt, who performed all the stunts in the film.

Thus, within a few years of the advent of a talking Zorro, Republic had produced a *singing* Zorro!

John Carroll, who actually sang the songs rather than using a voice double, had been born Julian LaFaye. He had run away from home at age 12 and had raced automobiles in Europe before coming to Hollywood in the 1930s. He began his career as a stuntman on the RKO lot before landing a lead role in *Hi Gaucho!*, a 1935 B picture. After *Zorro Rides Again*, which was his only serial, he went to MGM to star in a number of Westerns and war movies, culminating in *Plunderers of the Painted Flats* in 1959.

Directors William Witney and John English, who'd been involved with *Zorro Rides Again* in 1937, reunited two years later with stunt virtuoso Canutt and the original screenwriters for *Zorro's Fighting Legion*. The second Republic serial combined elements of the Western, police drama and the truly surreal—perhaps inspired by Man Ray's pioneer surrealist films of the 1920s, such as *The Mystery of the Chateau of Dice*.

The scene is set in Mexico in the 1858 to 1872 period when that country was governed by Benito Juarez. Zorro is pitted against Don Del Oro, a god adored by the Yaqui Indians, who in reality is an impostor seeking to steal Mexican gold being delivered to Juarez in Mexico City. The brains behind this treachery were played by Richard Alexander and Noah Beery. It is worth noting that Beery had played Sergeant Gonzales in the first screen Zorro in 1920 with Douglas Fairbanks. Beery's presence on the set was well publicized because he was now a 'big' star, but in fact all of his scenes in the entire serial are said to have been shot in a single day! Zorro ultimately manages to convince the Indians of the treachery of their false god, who perishes when he falls into a pit of flames after a spirited duel with Zorro.

One of the most astonishing stunts in this film was executed by Canutt, disguised as Zorro. Perched on the top of a stagecoach, he lets himself fall onto the galloping horses and then onto the ground, passes under the coach between the wheels, catches the back of the vehicle and climbs back onto the top. This stunt was borrowed 35 years later by Steven Spielberg and George Lucas for Harrison Ford in *Raiders of the Lost Ark*. A spectacular serial, *Zorro's Fighting Legion* benefited from the presence of Reed Hadley as Zorro and a remarkable musical score by William Lava and Cy Feuer.

Witney went on to direct such serials as *Dick Tracy Returns* and *The Lone Ranger*—both in 1938—as well as features that included *Hi-Ho Silver* (1940), *The Cool and the Crazy* (1958), *The Girls on the Beach* (1965), *Forty Guns to Apache Pass* (1966) and

Above: Reed Hadley seems to be in trouble in *Zorro's Fighting Legion*, released by Republic in 1939. This still appeared in the serial pictorial book. *Zorro Rides Again* featured the singing grandson of Zorro, played by John Carroll. Fans may recall the lobby card *(below)*, and the movie poster *(opposite page)*.

Darktown Strutters (1975). His milestones were, however, being chosen to direct the Roy Rogers serials in the late 1940s, *Master of the World* (1961) and *Zorro's Fighting Legion*, ironically his first serial as a director.

John English went on to direct a number of Gene Autry serials, as well as numerous Western features. His final films were *Silver Canyon* and *Valley of Fire*, both released in 1951.

Reed Hadley (born Reed Herring) went on to star in the 1941 Captain Marvel serial and in such classic war films as *Guadalcanal Diary* (1943) and *A Bell for Adano* (1945). He also was the voice of Red Ryder in the radio series, although he never played the Western hero on screen. In the 1950s, Hadley was a regular on such television series as *Racket Squad* and *Public Defender*. His last film was *The St Valentine's Day Massacre* in 1967.

ZORRO IN A MIGHTY MOTION PICTURE OF THE VIOLENT WEST!!

A REPUBLIC PICTURE

ZORRO

ZORRO RIDES AGAIN

starring
JOHN CARROLL and **DUNCAN RENALDO**
with HELEN CHRISTIAN and All-Star Cast
Directors WILLIAM WITNEY and JOHN ENGLISH
Written by BARRY SHIPMAN · JOHN RATHMELL · FRANKLYN ADREON · RONALD DAVIDSON · MORGAN COX
A REPUBLIC PICTURE

The Mark of Zorro

Fox Makes Its Mark

When Republic began to produce its B movie Zorros, the legend was still strong enough to interest the major studios, specifically Twentieth Century-Fox, whose nickname 'Fox' was a literal translation of the name of the character they sought to immortalize. Across town, rival Warner Brothers had been having a great deal of success with a series of adventure films—such as the immortal *Adventures of Robin Hood* (1938), featuring its handsome leading man, Errol Flynn. Twentieth Century-Fox was also anxious to cash in on the 'big adventure' genre. They had Tyrone Power under contract; all they needed was a good vehicle for him. Enter Zorro.

In terms of production, Twentieth Century-Fox's 1940 remake of *The Mark of Zorro* resembled the Douglas Fairbanks original of two decades earlier in content as it resembled the Warners/Flynn *Robin Hood* in its lavish production values.

When Fairbanks had picked up his copy of *The Curse of Capistrano* in 1920, filmmaking was a rudimentary art, with productions characterized by flat sets, badly balanced film stock and *no* sound. In 1940, however, Hollywood was well into its golden age. The films made in the 1939-1942 period still rank among the best ever produced. The list is awesome: *Gone with the Wind, Citizen Kane, The Wizard of Oz, The Maltese Falcon, Yankee Doodle Dandy* and *Casablanca*. The high quality of these films is due in large measure to their scripts and the casts, but their enduring quality is also attributable to the talents of the production and technical crews. Thus it was that *The Mark of Zorro*, directed by Rouben Mamoulian—who had also directed Greta

Garbo in *Queen Christina* in 1933—is today seen as one of the yardsticks by which all other Zorros are measured.

Fox did everything it could to guarantee a success that would parallel Warners Brothers' *Robin Hood*. In fact, Darryl F Zanuck, the president of Twentieth Century-Fox, had even wanted to get Flynn to play Zorro, but Jack Warner wouldn't let him go. It is probably just as well. Today, we can remember the two films as distinct and separate entities, albeit of similar genres: Flynn opposite Olivia de Havilland as Maid Marian and Power opposite Linda Darnell as the lovely Lolita. Fox even went so far as to hire both Basil Rathbone and Eugene Pallette to recreate in Southern California the same characters—villain and father confessor— they'd created in Sherwood Forest. Rathbone—most often remembered today for his 1939-1946 Sherlock Holmes series of feature films—was as perfect as the villain Captain Esteban Pasquale as was Tyrone Power as Zorro. Perhaps more so. Pallette's Father Felipe was a virtual clone of his Friar Tuck in *Robin Hood*, but it worked beautifully.

Himself an accomplished fencer, Rathbone contributed a profound realism to the duel scenes. One particular sequence—the final showdown—goes a long way in its combination of humor and action to climax the film. Before the duel, Rathbone and Power—also an excellent fencer—warm up with a few preliminary exercises. Esteban, sure of his superiority, slices through the top of a candle. He is soon imitated by Zorro, who pretends to

Above: The Camulos Ranch, located near Buenaventura, was a typical Mission-era ranch home of a pioneering Spanish family. *Opposite page:* Tyrone Power in mask, hat and saber for the Twentieth Century-Fox production of *The Mark of Zorro*.

TYRONE
POWER ★ DARNELL
LINDA

THE MARK OF
Zorro

20th CENTURY-FOX Encore Hit!

PRODUCED BY RAYMOND GRIFFITH
DIRECTED BY ROUBEN MAMOULIAN

SCREEN PLAY BY JOHN TAINTOR FOOTE · ADAPTATION BY GARRETT FORT
BASED ON THE STORY BY JOHNSTON McCULLEY

miss. Esteban bursts out laughing, but his mirth is short lived. Zorro had cut the candle so neatly that it had remained in place without falling.

Mamoulian's brilliant direction was complemented by the breathtaking cinematography of Arthur Miller and the fabulous sets of Richard Day and Joseph Wright, which all combined to make this definitive Zorro a box office hit as well as a lasting film classic.

Among the accomplishments of the off-stage team the score composed by Max Steiner is most memorable. Born in Vienna in 1888, Steiner had been a child prodigy at the Imperial Academy, had studied under Gustav Mahler and became a conductor at age 16. Steiner arrived in the United States in 1914 and found his niche on Broadway conducting and orchestrating the works of Florenz Ziegfeld and Victor Herbert.

With the advent of "talking pictures," movies not only had voice, but music as well. Like many of his contemporaries, Steiner saw his future in Hollywood and he went west in 1929. By the time he was tapped to score *The Mark of Zorro*, Steiner had already made his own mark with music for over a dozen films including *Gone With The Wind* (1939) and *The Informer* for which he won the 1935 Academy Award.

Ultimately, Steiner scored more than 200 films, including *Casablanca* (1943), *A Summer Place* (1959) and *Key Largo* (1948), and he won two more Oscars (from 15 nominations) as well as the top prize at the 1948 Venice Film Festival.

A year after *The Mark of Zorro*, Rouben Mamoulian went on to direct Tyrone Power again in *Blood and Sand* and the film version of *Summer Holiday* in 1948. He worked on Broadway in *Carousel* and *Oklahoma* before returning to Hollywood in 1957 to direct Fred Astaire and Cyd Charisse in *Silk Stockings*.

Tyrone Power went on to star in such adventure films as *A Yank in the RAF* (1942) and *An American Guerrilla in the Philippines*

Opposite page: With the dashing Tyrone Power as Zorro and the lovely Linda Darnell as Lolita, Twentieth Century-Fox hoped to compete with Warner Brothers' Robin Hood (starring Errol Flynn) in the adventure genre. Both movies have become classics. *Left:* Zorro returns to the pulp pages in 1940, this time reincarnated as Tyrone Power, in this 'smart' Hollywood rag. *Above:* movie posters for *The Mark of Zorro* showcased the dual talents of Zorro: a lover and a duelist. The 1940 remake ensured Zorro's place as a cult hero for all time.

(1950). He kept fairly active in the 1950s, although he never achieved the pinnacle of stardom for which he had seemed destined in the era before World War II. His years with the Marine Corps during the war are said to have aged him beyond the youthful 'leading man' look that he had exuded in the 1930s. His last film, *Witness for the Prosecution*, appeared in 1958, the year that he died.

Basil Rathbone went on to a highly successful stint as master sleuth Sherlock Holmes, while Linda Darnell immortalized the role of the sultry temptress in the 1948 film, *Forever Amber*, and later starred as the love interest in a number of American and European adventure films in the 1950s and 1960s.

With the 'remake' of *The Mark of Zorro* by Twentieth Century-Fox in 1940, there was no doubt that Zorro had taken his place alongside Robin Hood in the realm of cult heroes, not just for the time being, but for all time.

The Serials Roll

Even as Fox's *Zorro* made its mark, Johnston McCulley moved to lake Arrowhead to write more about Zorro, and Republic continued to produce Zorro serials. In 1944, Republic produced *Zorro's Black Whip*, in which the studio screenwriters imagined a *female* Zorro. We'd seen impersonators, impostors and three generations of Señor Zorros. Now there was a *Señorita* Zorro! Linda Stirling, who was then the queen of Republic serials, played Barbara Meredith, a young journalist who changed into a mysterious masked rider called 'The Black Whip' to avenge her brother's assassination by an outlaw band that was spreading terror across the Idaho range. *The Black Whip* was really more of a showcase for Stirling than a memorable Zorro film.

Later, Republic's writers revived the concept of a 'Zorro Jr' in *The Son of Zorro* (1947), which starred George Turner—who landed the job by claiming that his mother was related to the real

Zorro—and then introduced his *ghost* in *The Ghost of Zorro* (1949), with former circus aerialist and stuntman Clayton Moore in the title role. Moore, who had starred in the serials *Dick Tracy Returns* (1938) and *Jesse James Rides Again* (1947), soon went on to pick up the mask again as he stepped into the role for which he'll always be remembered, television's Lone Ranger, a masked avenger loosely based on Zorro.

Ever searching for twists on the winning Zorro formula, Republic created yet another in the pantheon of Zorro look-alikes with *Don Daredevil Rides Again* (1951), which starred Ken Curtis (later known for his portrayal of 'Festus' on CBS's long-running Western, *Gunsmoke*) and was distributed with the 'Zorro' name

Below: Linda Stirling appeared as the only female Zorro in Republic's *Zorro's Black Whip. Opposite page:* Basil Rathbone as Esteban Pasquale, the villain and George Ragas as his bumbling underling, Sergeant Gonzales, in *The Mark of Zorro*.

IBIS-films présente

George **TURNER**
Peggy **STEWART**
Roy **BARCROFT**
Edward **CASSIDY**

Le **FILS DE ZORRO**

DE ZOON VAN ZORRO

Above: Zorro transcends international boundaries. The Old West is brought to Belgium in *Son of Zorro*. *Opposite page:* In the Republic 'B' movie, *Ghost of Zorro*, Clayton Moore, in the title role, first donned the black mask that later became his signature as television's Lone Ranger. Both masked men gallop in (Zorro on his black steed, Toronado, and the Lone Ranger on his white steed, Silver) to anonymously champion the weak and oppressed, with no need of thanks

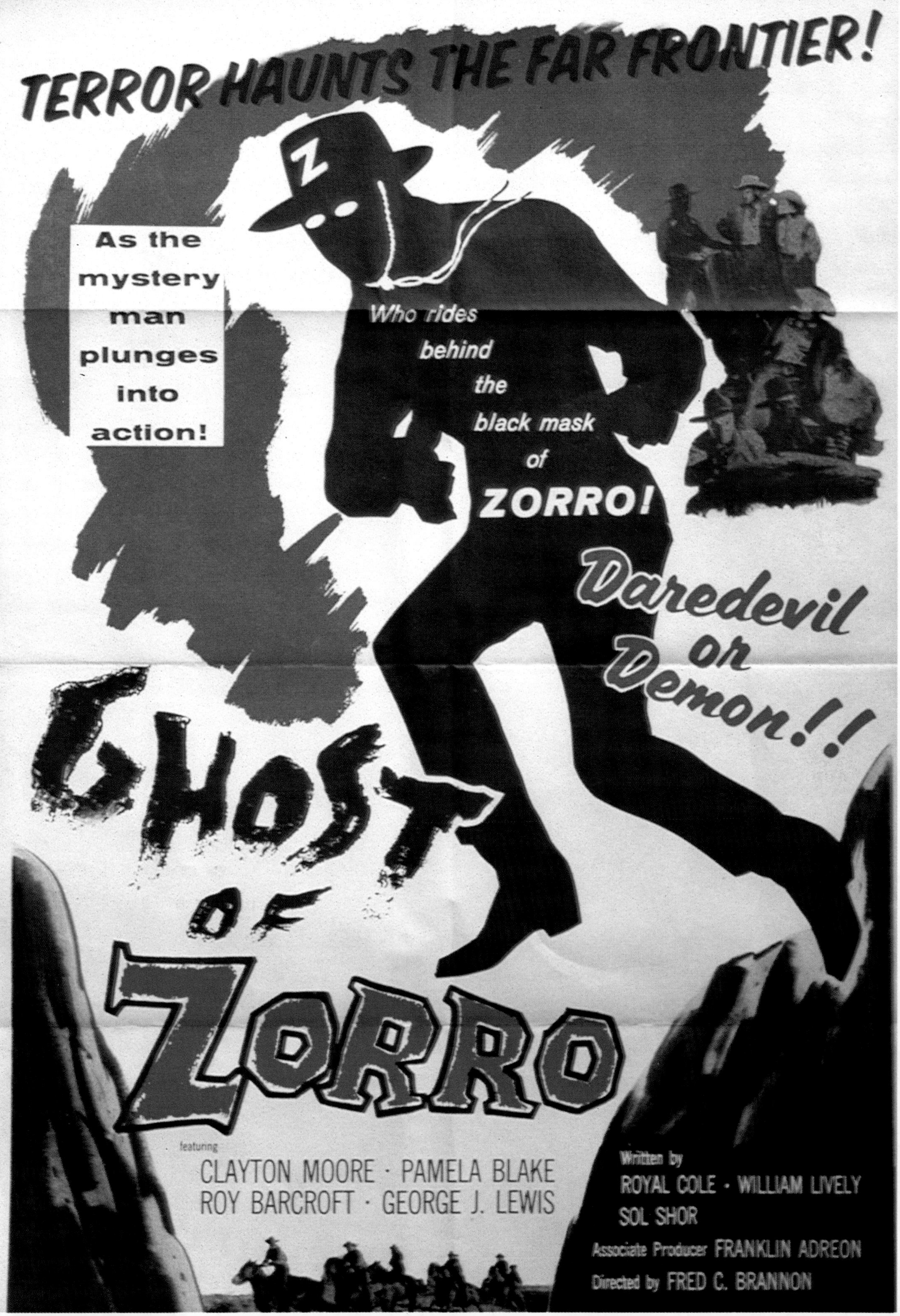

PUBLICITY

A REPUBLIC SERIAL IN **12** CHAPTERS

1 Col. x 26 Lines   103

"GHOST OF ZORRO"   (2C)

← "GHOST OF ZORRO"... Republic's thrill-packed new chapter play, starts this............... afternoon at the .... Theatre. Featured are Pamela Blake, Clayton Moore in the title role, and George J. Lewis.

California's Cold Wave Hits Movie-Making Troupe

Republic's exciting new serial, "Ghost of Zorro," a chapter of which plays each .... at the.................. Theatre, was filmed during the coldest and stormiest wheather experienced in California in more than 25 years. Much of the action was filmed at Iverson's Motion Picture Ranch, high in the rocky hills, where the wind howled so loudly the actors couldn't hear the shouts of the director. It was so cold, the actors couldn't speak their lines because of the chattering of their teeth. Making a serial is tough at best because of the rigorous routines involved, but it just so happened that this particular one was made during California's most "unusual" weather. It was the week just preceding California's first snowfall since way back in 1932, and the mercury was never lower.

Clayton Moore and Pamela Blake have the leading roles in the thrill-packed film and Roy Barcroft, Eugene Roth and George Lewis are featured in top roles.

"GHOST OF ZORRO"   (2B)

← FIERCE STRUGGLE... Clayton Moore battles Dale Van Sickel in a scene from Republic's excitement-crammed episoder, "Ghost Of Zorro," now playing each .... afternoon at the........................ Theatre.

Serial Actors Outfitted With Non-Skid Shoes

Working in the action-packed, Republic's serial, "Ghost of Zorro," playing each.............. at the............. Theatre, was so dangerous that all the actors had specially-made non-skid soles on their shoes. This helped prevent them from slipping on rocks and falling when climbing through hazardous, mountainous terrain. Shoes fitted with these special soles also make it easier for a man to keep on his feet during the many terrific slug fests involved in the exciting chapter play.

Handsome, athletic Clayton Moore co-stars with lovely Pamela Blake in the film which Fred Brannon directed for Republic.

1 Col. x 14 Lines   101

A REPUBLIC SERIAL IN **12** CHAPTERS

1 Col. x 14 Lines   102

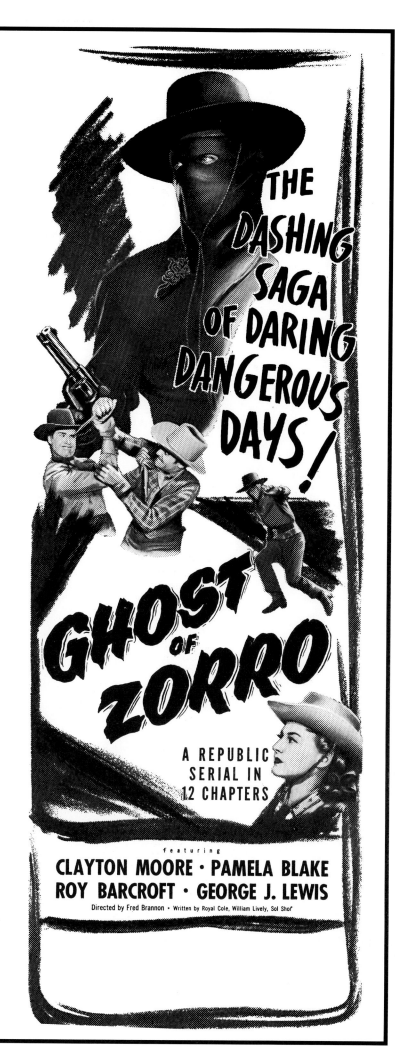

THE DASHING SAGA OF DARING DANGEROUS DAYS!

GHOST of ZORRO

A REPUBLIC SERIAL IN 12 CHAPTERS

featuring

CLAYTON MOORE · PAMELA BLAKE
ROY BARCROFT · GEORGE J. LEWIS

Directed by Fred Brannon · Written by Royal Cole, William Lively, Sol Shor

in France under the title *Zorro the Black Devil*. In this film, a lawyer dons the uniform of a lawman to come to the aid of his cousin and exploited farmers. In 1954, the last Republic serial to feature a simulated Zorro, *The Man with the Steel Whip*, was produced. In this film, El Latigo, a young rancher named Jerry Randall, played by Richard Simmons, brings peace between California farmers and the Indians.

Father Comes Home

Even as he was completing screenplays for Republic and cranking out his annual Zorro episode for *All Story Weekly*, Johnston McCulley continued to work on numerous projects for several small film companies, for whom he mostly wrote original Westerns. In 1937, he had done *Rootin' Tootin' Rhythm* and *Red Rope* for Republic. For Monogram he wrote *Rose of the Rio Grande* (1938); *Outlaws of Stampede Pass* (1943); *Raiders of the Border* (1944) and *South of the Rio Grande* (1945). He also scripted the 1942 serial *Overland Mail* for Universal, and after the war he wrote *Don Ricardo Returns* (1946) for PRC and *The Mark of the Renegade* (1951).

By early 1941, McCulley was ready to devote himself fully to the acclaimed hero he had fathered. Only World War II would briefly interrupt his efforts. McCulley moved in with his daughter and only child, Maurine, now a well known portrait painter, who had a studio at Strawberry Flats high in the Lake Arrowhead country of the San Bernadino Mountains. He rolled up his sleeves and went to work.

After completing one story—*Zorro Hunts by Night*—for *Cavalier Classics* in September 1940, he returned to *All Story Weekly* (now merged with *Argosy*) in January 1941. Coming on the heels of Fox's successful *The Mark of Zorro*, McCulley's *The Sign of Zorro* was his fourth—and last—big multipart blockbuster series for the magazine that had midwifed the birth of Zorro 22 years before. The series ran in five episodes, ending in the February 22 issue.

Any plans that *Argosy* and McCulley may have had for a follow-up to *The Sign of Zorro* (McCulley *never* wrote a story entitled *The Mark of Zorro*) were shelved because of the United States' entry into World War II. By the time he picked up his pen again in 1944 to begin what was to be the most productive eight years of his storytelling career, McCulley had scrapped not only the multipart story concept but also his publisher. By the mid-1940s, the pulps had gone from weekly to monthly because of wartime paper rationing, and McCulley went to *West* magazine, writing short stories as he had done briefly in the 1930s.

Beginning in July 1944, McCulley would write over 50 stories for *West*, more than triple what he'd done for *All Story Weekly/Argosy*. He published three stories in 1944, and thereafter, through 1950, he averaged eight per year, hitting a peak of 12 stories in 1947.

After the war, McCulley also wrote *Madcap of the Broken Wheel*, which appeared in *Golden West Romances* in 1950 and featured the heroine Molly Murphy. Five years later, he published what was to be his last novel, *The Devil's Doubloons*.

In 1949, Republic released *Ghost of Zorro* in 12 chapters. These ad slicks were sized for almost any type of newspaper column, and provided by the studio to the theaters. Sometimes the theaters were charged a dime for this advertising service. Short articles about the making of the film or the stars' romantic entanglements were often included to generate interest in the film.

TYRONE
POWER

Linda
DARNELL

in

THE
MARK
OF
Zorro

PRODUCED BY RAYMON
DIRECTED BY ROUBEN

Above: This lobby card for *The Mark of Zorro* has nary a sword to be seen. Tyrone Power romances Linda Darnell *sans* mask. *Right:* In addition to writing screen-plays and his annual Zorro installment, McCulley produced one story for *Cavalier Classics*— *Zorro Hunts by Night.*

Below: In 1937 Zorro rode again, this time on airplanes and automobiles. John Carroll as Zorro wielded revolvers instead of a blade, and occasionally burst into song. *Opposite page:* In the *Ghost of Zorro*, Clayton Moore played the figure upon whom his later role, the Lone Ranger was loosely based.

Beware the dreaded Z

ZORRO RIDES AGAIN

starring JOHN CARROLL and DUNCAN RENALDO with HELEN CHRISTIAN and All-Star Cast

Directors WILLIAM WITNEY and JOHN ENGLISH   Written by BARRY SHIPMAN·JOHN RATHMELL·FRANKLYN ADREON   A REPUBLIC PICTURE
RONALD DAVIDSON·MORGAN COX

JULY

CAVALIER
Classics

10¢

GEORGE CHALLIS
F. V. W. MASON
JOHNSTON McCULLEY
THEODORE ROSCOE

Tizzo, Italy's Firebrand –
Zorro of Old California –
Dougall the Scotch Buccaneer – *these heroes
ca ved the path of history with their brave blades*

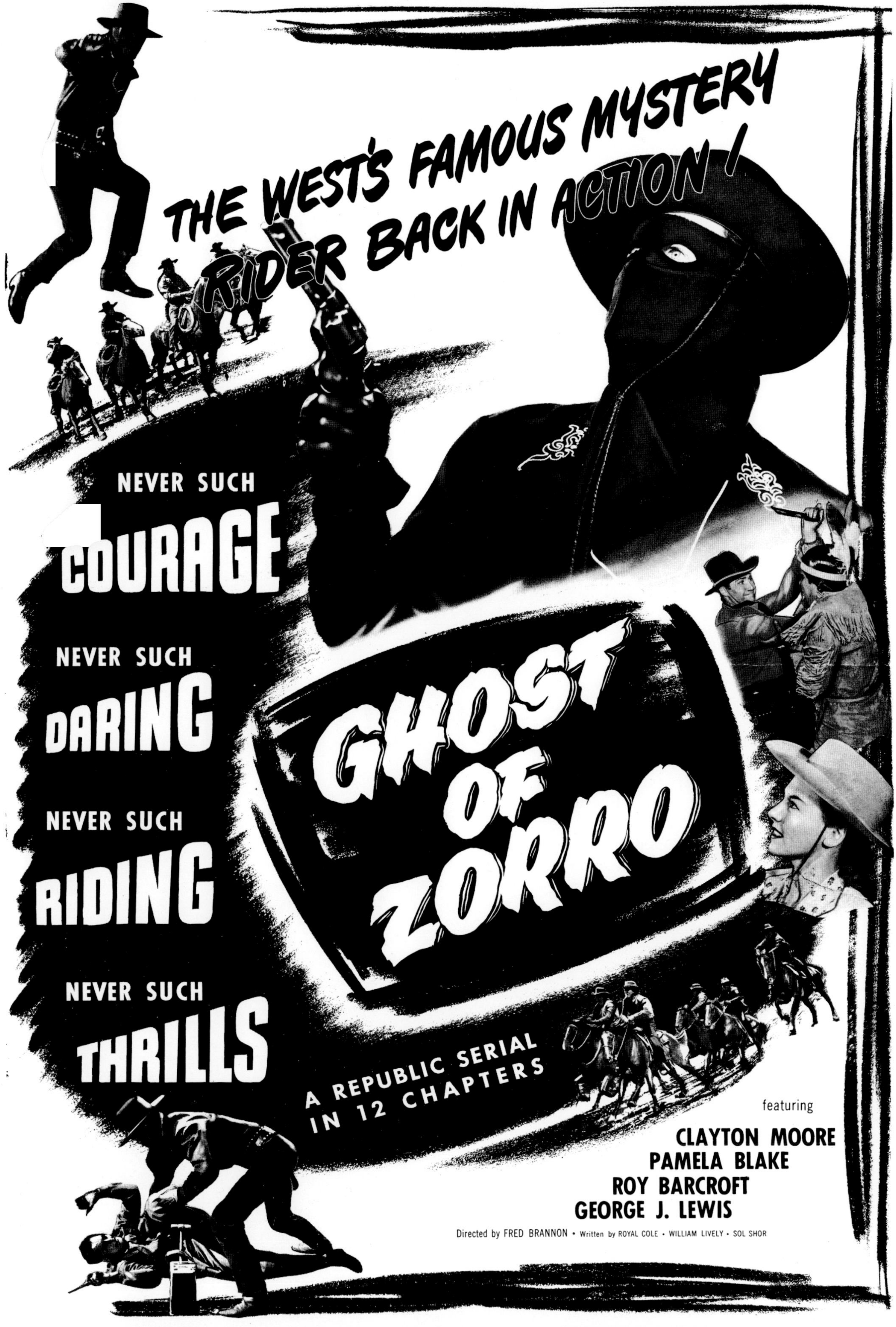
THE WEST'S FAMOUS MYSTERY
RIDER BACK IN ACTION!
NEVER SUCH
COURAGE
NEVER SUCH
DARING
NEVER SUCH
RIDING
NEVER SUCH
THRILLS
GHOST OF ZORRO
A REPUBLIC SERIAL
IN 12 CHAPTERS
featuring
CLAYTON MOORE
PAMELA BLAKE
ROY BARCROFT
GEORGE J. LEWIS
Directed by FRED BRANNON • Written by ROYAL COLE • WILLIAM LIVELY • SOL SHOR

The Guy Williams Era

Out of the night when
    the full moon is bright
Comes the horseman
    known as Zorro.
This bold renegade carves
    a 'Z' with his blade,
A 'Z' which stands for Zorro.
                —Henry Bruns and Norman Foster
                (the theme song from *Zorro*)

The Age of Television

The Twentieth Century-Fox version of *The Mark of Zorro* released in 1940 can perhaps be regarded as the single most highly regarded masterpiece of the Zorro legend. However, the work of Guy Williams who *was* Zorro for 78 television episodes between 1957 and 1959 would be the phenomenon which indelibly ingrained the image of Zorro into the public consciousness of the United States and the world.

By 1957, it had been eight years since Republic's last Zorro serial, *The Ghost of Zorro*, and three years since *The Man with the Steel Whip*, Republic's film which featured a Zorro 'impersonator.' By now, television, which had been on the air in the United States for nearly a decade, had come of age, influencing every facet of the American lifestyle like no other entertainment medium before it.

Meanwhile, in 1950, Johnston McCulley had sold all of his rights in the Zorro property to Mitchell Gertz, a prominent Hollywood theatrical agent. Gertz then wasted no time in convincing Walt Disney that Zorro would be perfect for the new and exploding medium of television, and he assigned all his rights in Zorro to the Disney Company in 1952. It would take five more years for the show to reach the air.

After the spectacular success of the 1955 and 1956 films *Davy Crockett, King of the Wild Frontier* and *Davy Crockett and the River Pirates*, which they had turned into a merchandising extravaganza, Walt Disney Studios were eager to develop more in the adventure film genre, and Zorro was among the characters that were considered.

Above: Guy Williams, Zorro in 78 television episodes, had previously supplemented his New York stage income by doing toothpaste commercials. *Opposite page:* Williams, along with Johnston McCulley, creator of Zorro and author of well over a hundred pulp fiction tales, peruse the story that started it all.

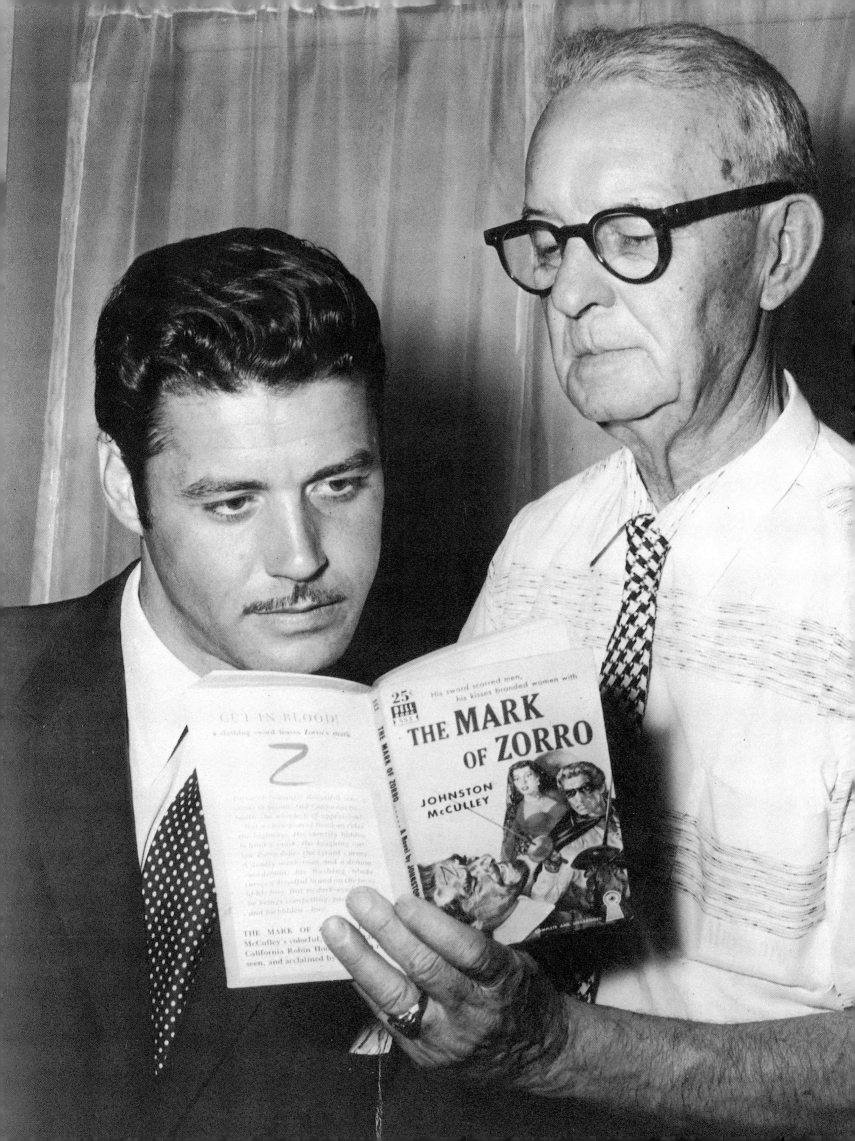

Strangely, Disney, concerned that no adventure series could ever do as well as *Davy Crockett*, chose to film the entire Zorro series in black and white. Nevertheless, they hired Hollywood veteran director Norman Foster, who had been active in the film industry since directing *Gentlemen of the Press* in 1929, and who had directed Fess Parker in both of Disney's blockbuster *Davy Crockett* films.

Casting the lead character presented a key challenge for Disney. The studio had decided to forego a 'name' star and hire a relative unknown. The casting call went out and over a hundred would-be Pimpernels lined up for the screening process. Finally, the decision was made. Zorro would be a 33-year-old actor named Guy Williams.

Born Guido Catalano in 1923 in New York City to Italian-American parents, the young Williams had attended the Peekskill Military Academy in New York before going to Hollywood in 1952. He had been signed to a one-year contract with Universal International where he landed a bit part in the Ronald Reagan film, *Bedtime for Bonzo,* and another role in *I Was a Teenage Werewolf,* starring Michael Landon as the werewolf. After shooting was completed on *Werewolf,* Guido, who had taken the stage name Guy Williams, returned to work on the New York stage, supplementing his income by doing toothpaste commercials. He had only just set foot back in Hollywood in 1957 when he was offered an audition for Zorro.

At one point, Williams had thought it might be a good idea to take lessons from a fencing master. This training paid off handsomely for him, as he was able to pass the Zorro audition hands down. This quality of a swashbuckler, together with his talent as a comedian, made the 6'3" Guy Williams an ideal Zorro.

Opposite page, below and bottom left: Mitchell Gertz created this mock-up after purchasing the Zorro rights from McCulley. It eventually helped him sell Zorro to Disney. *Right:* The first paperback edition, published in the 1940s. Zorro made his first appearance in this story, originally titled *The Curse of Capistrano.* Note the red-headed Zorro.

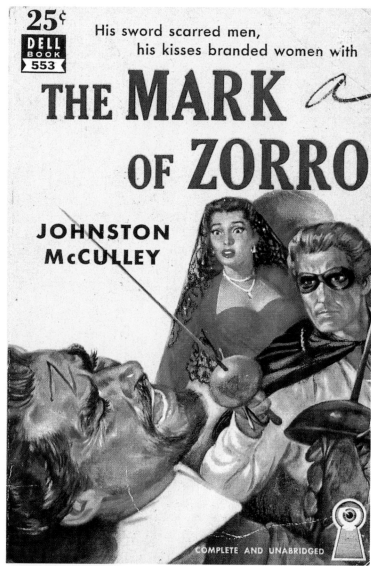

25¢ DELL BOOK 553

His sword scarred men, his kisses branded women with

THE MARK OF ZORRO

JOHNSTON McCULLEY

COMPLETE AND UNABRIDGED

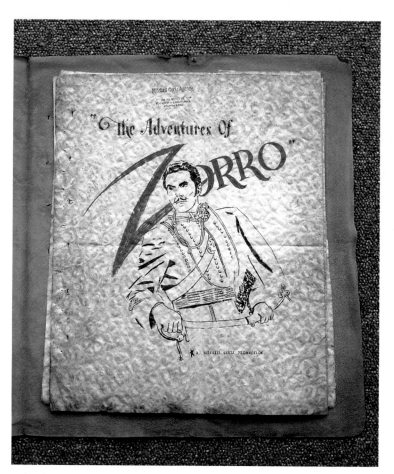

"The Adventures Of *Zorro*"

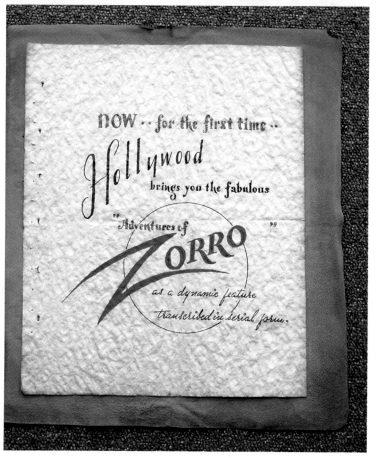

NOW .. for the first time .. *Hollywood* brings you the fabulous "Adventures of *Zorro*" as a dynamic feature transcribed in serial form.

Above: For millions of television viewers, Guy Williams *was* Zorro: tall, dark, handsome and dashing (shown here with Britt Lomond as Monastario).

Opposite page: Williams was an unknown when *Zorro* appeared in 1957. Luckil Williams had fenced before, because Disney decided that only *real* foils would be use

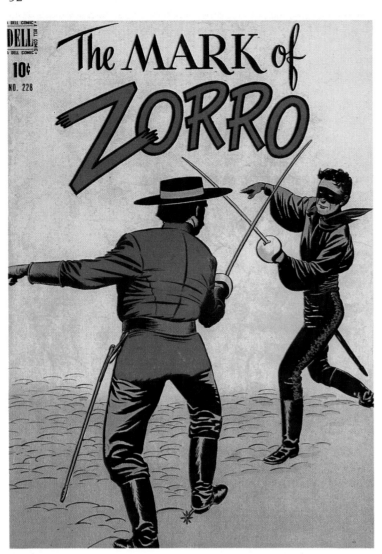

Contrary to most cinematic duels that are done with blunted foils, the sensational confrontations in the television series would be staged with *real* swords whose points were not protected. Under these conditions, the hiring criteria for the role required an actor with faultless ability in the subtle art of swordsmanship.

Disney's television series, simply entitled *Zorro*, was constructed so that while each of the 78 episodes could stand alone (that is, every episode was satisfying in and of itself), most belonged to four-, five- or even 13-episode sequences of continuing plotlines. After Zorro films set in such diverse venues as Mexico, Spain and even New York, it was a relief to have Disney set his Zorro back in Southern California. As the saga opened, young Don Diego, at the request of his father, returned from Spain to his native California, where the noble dons and the peasants were being oppressed by the evil Captain Monastorio, Commander of the cuartel of Los Angeles. Passing himself off in public as lazy and ineffective, Don Diego—helped by his mute valet Bernardo—disguised himself as Zorro to oppose the cruel Captain and his flunky, the fat and incompetent Sergeant Garcia, who provided the comic relief.

With characteristic thoroughness, the same ideal that would compel the Disney studio to use real swords in fight sequences, led them to assemble a production team that included some of the most experienced Zorro hands in Hollywood.

Fred Cavens, the fencing master who had coached both Douglas Fairbanks and Tyrone Power, was brought in, as was Dave Sharp, who later worked as a stuntman in the Republic serials. William Lava, one of the composers for the score of *Zorro's Fighting Legions*, wrote the brilliant background music. This score

Top, left: The first Zorro comic book cover, released in 1949. *Opposite page:* A Disney-era comic book. With the advent of the 1957 Disney television series, Dell's Zorro took on the appearance of Guy Williams, the actor who portrayed Zorro. *Below:* This Zorro jigsaw puzzle is today worth $33 to a collector.

involved the use of a device reminiscent of *Peter and the Wolf* in which each character had his own instrumental *theme* that was played when he came on the scene. The vocal theme song, composed by George Bruns, with words by Norman Foster, was initially recorded with Mitch Miller and the Sandpipers. It also was featured on Hit Parade in 1958, thanks to a version sung by the Chordettes.

George J Lewis, previously seen in *Zorro's Black Whip* and *Ghost of Zorro*, played Zorro's father, Don Alejandro. Finally, Johnston McCulley himself was brought in to supervise the writing of the episodes.

The series was conceived in terms of 39-episode seasons, and ran for two seasons for a total of 78 shows. The first 39 were

These pages: One of the three versions of Zorro board games and a boxed costume. A collector could expect to receive $75-$175 for a game whose masks, sabers and capes are intact.

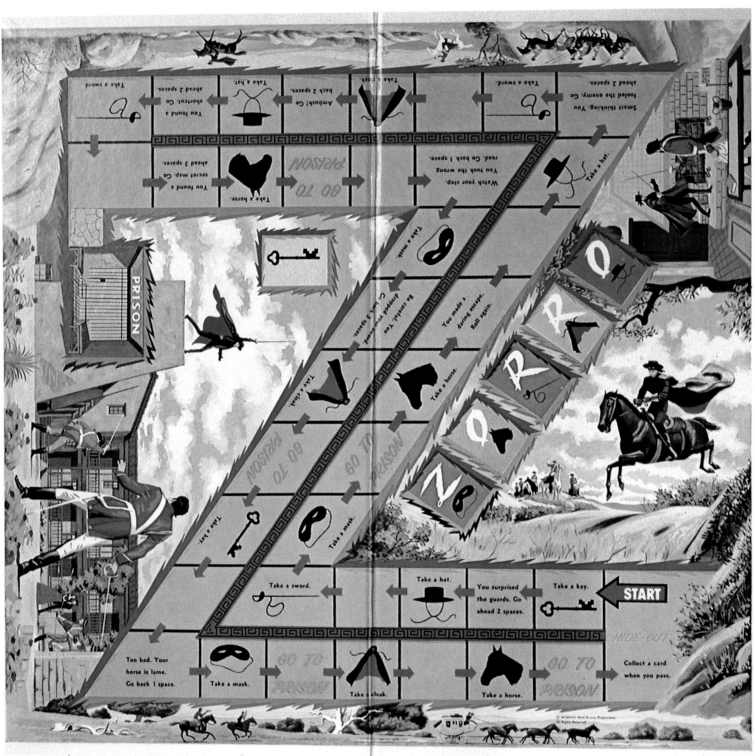

Ben Cooper Inc.
AUTHENTIC
WALT DISNEY ©
CHARACTER COSTUME
MASQUERADE COSTUMES

filmed for $3.2 million and the second for a lesser $2.7 million, because the sets already existed. Disney had built the half million dollar 'Zorro City' on its studio's back lot, which existed until about 1985.

The Guy Williams/Walt Disney *Zorro* had its debut on ABC on October 10, 1957 with an episode entitled *Presenting Señor Zorro*, and concluded its first season on July 3, 1958 with *Day of Decision*, although it was reprised in 13 weeks of reruns before the start of the fall season's new episodes. The second season began on October 9, 1958 with *Welcome to Monterey* and ended on July 2, 1959 with *Finders Keepers*.

The series attained one of the highest audience ratings of its

Left: Supporting actors were chosen for their dueling ability, because the foil tips were left unprotected for the sake of realism. *Below:* Henry Calvin as Sergeant Garcia was the bumbling foil to the suave Zorro. *Opposite page:* Zorro and his sword were as deadly as Cupid and his arrows; Williams carved a figurative 'Z' into the hearts of many women.

Inset: The box cover to the Zorro Action Set. Collectors receive $300—enough to buy the horse—for one complete with *(below)* everything needed to protect and defend like Zorro.

era. The only reason it was canceled was that Walt Disney wanted to move both *Zorro* and *Disneyland* from ABC to NBC but found *Zorro* impossible to move. NBC, whose logo was now the peacock with the multicolored tail, wanted to bill itself as the "all-color" network and *Zorro* was in black and white! Disney chose to cancel *Zorro* rather than to stay on ABC.

When McCulley died on November 23, 1958 at the age of 79, it was amidst a height of Zorro popularity that he could not have imagined four decades earlier when he was inspired to create the caballero from L.A.

Mitchell Gertz died in 1961, and in 1967 Disney reassigned its rights in Zorro to the Gertz estate. Thus, to this day, all rights in the property of Zorro are controlled by the Gertz family through Zorro Productions, Inc. of Berkeley, California, whose president is Mitchell Gertz's son, John Gertz.

Meanwhile, the Disney television show had quickly spawned a Zorro craze among the youth of the nation. During the 1957-1958 school year, kids began writing Zs on their school

Below: Like father, like son. Guy Williams' son, Steve Catalano, joined millions of other boys and girls in the Zorro craze. The selling power of television was vastly different from just 35 years earlier, when theater owners were encouraged to draw crowds by hooking up with the local harness maker (*see page 22*) who would exhibit and, with luck, sell whips 'like those used in the picture'. Merchandise tie-ins were primarily used for promotional purposes, with the direct profits benefitting the lucky local merchant who sold beds like the one Doug Fairbanks used in the film.

Opposite page: Originally $4.14 (with tax), this record today brings $50 from collectors. Guy Williams and other original cast members were featured.

WALT DISNEY

FOUR ADVENTURES OF

Zorro

PRESENTING SEÑOR ZORRO
ZORRO FREES THE INDIANS
ZORRO AND THE GHOST
ZORRO'S DARING RESCUE

Guy Williams as ZORRO with other members of the original cast

notebooks and carrying Zorro lunchboxes to school. Merchandise tie-ins such as Zorro capes, hats, masks and swords sold briskly at toy stores. Among the most memorable toy products licensed by Disney in 1957 were the hat/cape/mask set produced by Ben Cooper, Inc of Brooklyn, and the official Zorro playset manufactured by Louis Marx & Company of New York. The latter included a metal hacienda with such accessories as a pellet-shooting cannon and an assortment of plastic 'action figures.' Marx also produced a duelling kit with a chalk-tipped sword for inscribing the signature 'Z'. T. Cohn of Brooklyn produced a metal target game with a black plastic rifle.

Jigsaw puzzles and numerous publications also appeared in 1958 and 1959. Western Publishing Company issued the Little Golden Book *Walt Disney's Zorro*, while Dell—the leading comic book publisher of the era—turned out a 15-installment series of stories which featured the talents of Alex Toth, who was destined to become one of the leading comic book illustrators in the United States. Parenthetically, Dell had issued Zorro comics as early as 1949, but the television tie-in was a tremendous windfall, so Dell's Zorro suddenly took on the appearance of Guy Williams. Between 1965 and 1968, Gold Key Comics would reprint nine books from the 1958 Dell comic book Zorro series.

Left, right and far right: Many games bore the mark—and likeness—of Zorro. *Below:* Topps produced a set of 88 Zorro trading cards from the 1957-1959 seasons of Walt Disney's *Zorro*. A complete set today fetches $200, as does the storage box. Cards with original wrappers bring $100 each.

Today, Zorro merchandise from the Disney era remains a favorite among collectors. If you can find a complete Marx playset in your attic you shouldn't have any problem getting at least $2500 for it. Meanwhile, the Marx sword, mask, whip, and ring set is now worth about $500, and a complete set of the 88 Topps cards would be worth about $400. In Appendix 5 there is a list of just some of the collectible Zorro items that could have been purchased in the late 50s and early 60s, along with their approximate values today.

The series won acclaim worldwide in all of the countries in which it was aired. In South America—most notably in Argentina—Guy Williams and Henry Calvin were viewed as national heroes. In France, the series inspired comic singer Henri Salvador to create one of his most popular songs. Today, in spite of the supremacy of color television, not a week goes by that a channel somewhere in the world does not air a black and white episode created for the Disney *Zorro* series. Indeed, while the episodes may be in black and white, they are also in gold—in more ways than one. This was, after all, the golden age of television. *The Honeymooners* and *I Love Lucy* were also filmed in black and white.

After the *Zorro* series ended in 1959, Disney kept Guy Williams and much of the production staff on the payroll through

Left and below: Zorro plastic dolls were sold separately or in tandem with Annette Funicello cut-outs. The Mouseketeer came complete with guitar, tennis racquet and ears. The swashbuckler came armed with guitar, sword, and pistol. *Opposite page:* Guy Williams brandishing his sword in a Disney publicity photo.

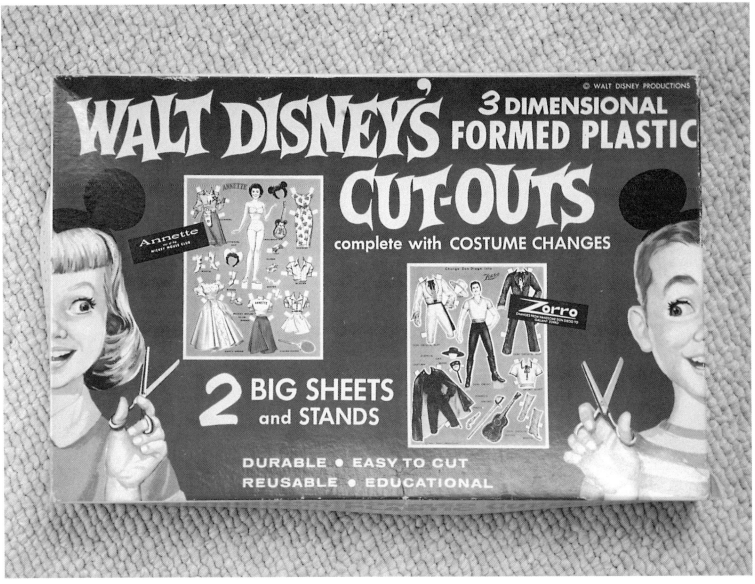

DIEGO'S DEFEAT

CHALLENGE FOR DIEGO

SOLDIER AND SCHOLAR

THE QUESTION

ZORRO'S PRISONER

THE CAPITAN'S TRIUMPH

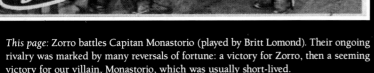

This page: Zorro battles Capitan Monastorio (played by Britt Lomond). Their ongoing rivalry was marked by many reversals of fortune: a victory for Zorro, then a seeming victory for our villain, Monastorio, which was usually short-lived.

Clockwise from upper left: Monastorio has both the swords and Don Diego has none; Diego fixes his tie; 'We have these in your size'; when boys rough-house someone always gets hurt; Zorro gives Monastorio a tip; class bully and teacher's pet.

THE EVIL SCHEME

DIEGO MEETS "ZORRO"

DIEGO'S HOMECOMING

GARCIA'S WARNING

DIEGO THE WEAKLING

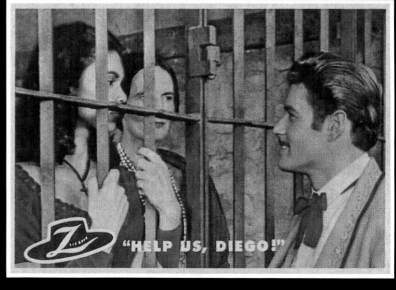

"HELP US, DIEGO!"

Clockwise from upper left: The cruel Monastorio gleefully plotting his evil deeds, but the audience knows that Zorro, fighting on the side of good, will triumph. Diego contends with a bogus Zorro; Sergeant Garcia throws his weight around; does Don

Diego dare to deliver a duo of damsels in distress?; if Diego wishes to impress this young woman, he should leave off his serenade, don his black suit and avenge the oppressed; father and son suit each other.

1961 for public appearances and for four hour-long Zorro specials: *El Bandito* (aired on October 30, 1960), *Adios El Cuchillo* (aired on November 6, 1960), *The Postponed Wedding* (aired on New Year's Day in 1961) and *Auld Acquaintance*, (aired on April 2, 1961).

Two films, *Zorro the Avenger* and *The Sign of Zorro* were also released. Prepared originally for release in Japan in 1958 and 1959, these 'films' were actually compilations of episodes from the television series. *The Sign of Zorro* was taken from the first half dozen episodes, while *Zorro, the Avenger* was episode 27 tacked on to precede episodes 35 through 39. Williams went on to star in *Captain Sinbad* in Italy and *Damon und Pythias* in Germany before returning to Hollywood, where he auditioned for the role of Adam Cartwright on *Bonanza* that ultimately went to Pernell Roberts. After several guest star spots, he landed a role in 1964 opposite June Lockhart (best known for her role as Timmy's mother in the *Lassie* television series) in the series *Lost in Space*.

Just as Johnston McCulley was never able to repeat his Zorro success with any of the other heroes he created, Guy Williams was never able to secure a role comparable to Zorro. Fess Parker, who had played the title role in Disney's *Davy Crockett* films, had made a great deal of money, and then invested his earnings in

Above: Two Zorro movies were made from compilations of episodes of the TV series, including *The Sign of Zorro*, featured in these two movie posters. *Right:* Zorro is saddled with the responsibility of admonishing those who 'stirrup' trouble. As long as he is there to coach them, law-breakers won't have free rein.

Above: Another post-cancellation compilation of Disney television serials was *Zorro, the Avenger*, released in 1958, which included episodes 29 and 35 through 39. *Below:* Zorro is pictured here with his faithful, mute manservant, played by Gene Sheldon, in a scene from *The Sign of Zorro*. The movie comprised episodes one through six of the series. *Opposite:* Zorro rides again from the TV to the theater.

Santa Barbara real estate, but Guy Williams was compelled to be philosophical about eventually losing his five-room house and the yacht that he'd possessed in his glory days.

In 1986, Williams was invited to Argentina, where the show was then playing. The country had welcomed him with open arms and he became a national cult figure if not an outright national hero. He spent the next several years in Zorro costume, entertaining and making appearances. He fell in love with Argentina's lifestyle and sprawling ranchos. He decided to remain, making only occasional return visits to the United States. Eventually, however, he became seriously reclusive. When he died of a heart attack in his Buenos Aires apartment in May 1989, his body was not found for a week.

The Minor Series

After such an enormous crescendo of celebrity, one had to wait many years before a new Zorro was produced for the home screen. In the made-for-television movie, *The Mark of Zorro*, produced in 1974 by the television department of Twentieth Century-Fox, director Don McDougall practically copied Rouben Mamoulian's 1940 *The Mark of Zorro* scene for scene. Filmed in color, as a television movie, Frank Langella's portrayal of Zorro earned the film great ratings.

Zorro was the subject of an animated, 13-episode Saturday morning television series produced by Filmation in 1981, and returned in a five-episode situation comedy entitled *Zorro and Son*. The latter was produced by Walt Disney in 1983 and aired on CBS—who'd requested that it be a sitcom rather than a dramatic series. It was aired in May and June of 1983, with Zorro and his son played by Henry Darrow and Paul Regina—it was seen as a

Zorro did not return to the small screen in a live-action series again until 1983. Awkwardly wearing a new mask of comedy, *Zorro and Son (above)* lasted only five episodes. *Above and opposite, left:* Bill Dana played Bernardo, the faithful manservant, in CBS' *Zorro and Son. Opposite, right:* Henry Darrow played the aristocratic Don Diego, father, partner and teacher to Don Carlos *(below)*, played by Paul Regina.

Zorro and Son: Henry Darrow *(right)* is the only actor to have been involved in three separate Zorro productions. Darrow was the voice of Zorro in the 1981 Filmation animated series, and has gone on to play Zorro's father. Paul Regina *(above, left)* is one in a distinguished line of Zorro scions, beginning in 1925 with Douglas Fairbanks, Sr a *Don Q, The Son of Zorro. Opposite page: Zorro and Son* was filmed on the same 'Zorro City' lot as the other Disney Zorro series, starring Guy Williams.

disappointing sequel to the 1958 television series. The film's action took place 25 years later when Don Diego Vega had aged and had a hard time filling his role of Zorro to combat the tyrant, Captain Paco Pico.

In this series, Don Diego reveals his secret identity to his son Carlos and teaches him to fence. Thereafter, father and son fight together. In a scene which sets the tone for the series, the villian proclaims: 'The old fox ain't what he used to be.' To which Zorro

Richard Beauchamp (*above*) played the bumbling Sergeant Sepulveda, the successor to the bumbling Sergeant Garcia in the 1957 series. *Opposite page:* The idea of Zorro working with his son also occurred with the 1925 sequel, *Don Q, The Son of Zorro*, in which Douglas Fairbanks played *both* father and son.

responds: 'What I lost in youth I gained in wisdom. If God wanted us always to jump to surmount obstacles, why did He invent stairs?' *Zorro and Son* was shot on the same Disney back lot, 'Zorro City,' as the 1957 series.

These pages: Zorro as he appeared in *The New Adventures of Zorro,* a Saturday morning animated television series. The series ran for 13 episodes in 1981. Produced by Filmation, the cel animation techniques used in the series were invented in the 1950s by Ub Iwerks, head of special processes at Walt Disney Studios. Iwerks modified a Xerox camera to transfer animators' drawings directly to the transparent sheets of celluloid known as cels. The cels are layered onto background drawings, and changed between exposures of individual frames to simulate motion. This allows for a looser style as well as saving time and money.

Below: All the great Western heroes had their trusty steeds: the Lone Ranger and Silver, Roy Rogers and Trigger, Gene Autry and Champion...Zorro and Toronado. Pictured here is Paul Regina's stunt double from the television series, *Zorro and Son.* Presumedly, the horse is the son of Toronado.

The World of Zorro

Universal Appeal

In the late 1940s, after the end of the Second World War, American films became a staple on European screens. As a result of four years of war and occupation, European domestic film industries were still moribund. Soon the matinee goers were eagerly awaiting the latest American serial drama, and they quickly made Zorro one of their idols. In Italy, France and Spain, the masked character became immensely popular.

In 1952, the first non-American film to feature him found Zorro in the parody *Il Sogno Di Zorro* (*The Sign of Zorro*), directed by Mario Soldati and starring Walter Chiari, one of the most popular comedians of the era, as Zorro. The story involved the cowardly son of a direct descendant of Zorro who'd been hit on the head and believed that he could eliminate an entire army single-handed. Vittorio Gassman played the role of the local tyrant, while the love interest was young Sofia Lazzaro, who would become a major celebrity a few years later under the name Sophia Loren.

In the 1960s, with the broadcast in Europe of the Disney television series, Zorro swiftly saturated the Mediterranean cinema. The timing had been auspicious, as the Italian 'spaghetti Western' was in its ascendancy, and more than a dozen Zorro films would be produced in Europe between 1961 and 1974. In 1963, Zorro found himself on the side of the Four Musketeers as he confronted Cardinal Richelieu in the seventeenth century in *Zorro E I Tre Moschiettieri* (*Zorro and the Three Musketeers*). He allied himself with Maciste and became king of Nogara in *Zorro*

The Disney series *Zorro* and the films inspired by it (*above*) sparked another Zorro craze. More than a dozen Zorro films were made in the 1960s (*opposite page*), while in Argentina Guy Williams became a living legend.

Contro Maciste (*Zorro Versus Maciste*) (1963). He was working for Queen Victoria against a tyrant who ruled over an English colony in Central America in *Zorro Alla Corte D'Inghilterra* (*Zorro in the Court of England*) (1969). He fought in opposition to Napoleonic troops who occupied Spain at the beginning of the nineteenth century in *Zorro Marchese Di Navarro* (*Zorro Marquis of Navarro*)

(1969). In 1962, 'Zorro' fought to return the grand duchy of Lusitania—ruled by a pretender—to its true hereditary ruler in *Zorro Alla Corte Di Spagnia* (*Zorro in the Court of Spain*).

The Europeans also chose to retain a California setting for *Il Venganza Del Zorro* (*Zorro's Revenge*) (1962), *L'Ombra Di Zorro* (*Zorro's Shadow*) (1963), *La Tre Spade Di Zorro* (*The Three Swordsmen of Zorro*) (1963) and *Il Giuramente Di Zorro* (*The Mark of Zorro*) (1965). For European audiences who couldn't conceive of California as a Latin country, the action was moved south of the border for several films set in Mexico, including *Zorro Il Ribelle* (*Zorro the Rebel*) (1966), *Zorro Il Dominatore* (*Zorro the Dominator*) (1969) and *Zorro La Maschera Della Vendettazi* (*Zorro the Mask of Revenge*) (1970).

However, the most important Zorro film made in Europe was *Zorro*, produced by and starring Alain Delon in 1974. As a sort of present from the French actor to his son, Delon's *Zorro* was a nostalgic glimpse of Delon's own adolescence, when, like many young people of his era, he was clamoring for adventures such as those of the American Pimpernel.

Zorro, the Gay Blade featured Ron Leibman and Brenda Vaccaro (above) and starred George Hamilton (*below and opposite*), with Lauren Hutton as an early feminist.

ZEXY, ZANY, ZENSATIONAL!

GEORGE HAMILTON IS *Zorro,*
THE GAY BLADE

MELVIN SIMON PRODUCTIONS PRESENTS A PETER MEDAK FILM
GEORGE HAMILTON IS ZORRO, THE GAY BLADE
Starring **LAUREN HUTTON BRENDA VACCARO** and **RON LEIBMAN**
Music Conducted and Adapted by **IAN FRASER** Director of Photography **JOHN A. ALONZO, A.S.C.**
Executive Producer **MELVIN SIMON** Screenplay by **HAL DRESNER**
Screen Story by **HAL DRESNER** and **GREG ALT & DON MORIARTY** and **BOB RANDALL**
Produced by **GEORGE HAMILTON** and **C.O. ERICKSON** Directed by **PETER MEDAK**

 PG PARENTAL GUIDANCE SUGGESTED
SOME MATERIAL MAY NOT BE SUITABLE FOR CHILDREN **READ THE LEISURE PAPERBACK** ©1981 TWENTIETH CENTURY-FOX

Opposite page: The Erotic Adventures of Zorro, was one of several films in which the
dual-identity duelist was more of a lover than a fighter. *Above:* Twentieth Century-

spoof 60 years later. George Hamilton plays Don Diego, and his identical twin
brother Bunny Wigglesworth; and their respective alter egos: Zorro and the

At the start of the 1970s, in two productions—one the Belgian *Aventures Galantes De Zorro* (*The Gallant Adventures of Zorro*) and the German-American *Erotic Adventures of Zorro*, the legendary hero added the boudoir to the scope of his exploits—without so much as taking off his mask. There were reportedly several other pornographic adaptations of the Zorro legend, but they have since disappeared without a trace.

The most outlandish parody was probably Mel Simon's *Zorro, The Gay Blade* (1980), which exploited the effeminate side of the double identity of Don Diego. The film was seen as Simon's follow-up to his 1979 satire *Love at First Bite* which featured George Hamilton as a comic Count Dracula. *The Gay Blade* would again star Hamilton in the lead role. When the heterosexual Zorro/Don Diego breaks his leg jumping from a balcony, his twin brother, the homosexual 'Don Diego,' known as Bunny Wigglesworth, picks up his sword. Hamilton, who was also co-producer, borrowed from the *Adventures of Don Juan* with Errol Flynn to interpret the roles of both Don Diego and Bunny Wigglesworth.

Left: George Hamilton as Bunny Wigglesworth, the 'swishbuckling' hero, assumes the identity of his (almost) identical twin brother, Zorro. Bunny brandishes a bullwhip instead of a sword. *Below:* The cape, mask and hat of Zorro are all the rage at a lavish masked ball thrown by Zorro's arch rival, the Alcalde, played by Ron Leibman. *Opposite page:* George Hamilton unmasked.

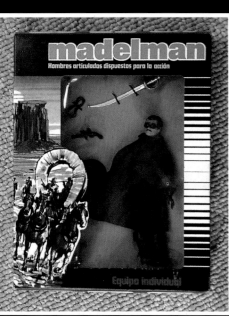

The collectibles of the future? The Zorro Productions licensing and merchandising blitz has brought out new Zorro toys world-wide. *At top:* A mask of Sergeant Garcia on the left, and at right, a masked mask of Zorro himself. *Above:* A Zorro plastic action figure. *Right:* Zorro cookies. *Opposite page, top:* Zorro books, and finally, a Zorro book bag in which to carry them all *opposite page, below.*

The Comic Strip Zorro

The international appeal of Zorro is matched by few other fictional American heroes. Indeed, it was in *Italy* during the Second World War that the first comic strip Zorro appeared. Designed by A Valli, it was later picked up by Zamperoni, and eventually Penego in the news paper *L'Audace*. It is interesting— and ironic—that this enemy of tyrants made his mark while Mussolini's fascists held Italy in their iron grip.

In 1939, in the French weekly *Jumbo*, Zorro, 'the man with the whip,' made his first appearance under the pencil of Tori, then in 1940 under that of Gal (Georges Langlais), who would become a well-known illustrator in the late 1940s and 1950s. Meanwhile, between 1941 and 1942, the Italian version appeared in France in the *Victory* collection of the Sagedition. Zamperoni's Zorro appeared in Sagedition and the paper, *Adventures,* in Italy in 1947. At the same time in France, the Editions Mondiales (World Editions) introduced a Zorro with superb illustrations by Gire. In 1949, five episodes appeared in the Hurrah collection under these evocative titles: *La Machine Infernale* (*The Infernal Machine*), *Zorro A La Rescousse* (*Zorro to the Rescue*) and *Les Adventurers Du Rail* (*The Rail Adventurers*). *L'Intrepide*, *Le Vengeur Masque* and *Le Protege De Zorro* were published in 1948-1949 by Editions Mondiales, illustrated by Bob Dan (Robert Dansler) with scripts by Georges Fronval, two big names in European comic strips of the 1950s.

Andre Oulie's version lasted for years and filled many thousands of pages in the large format weekly *Jeudi Magazine* (*Thursday Magazine*). This periodical, published by the Societe Francaise de Presse Illustree, later became *L'Invincible*, which evolved into a monthly paperback after 1953.

Oulie's Zorro frequently dressed in 'the traditional colors of the night,' which was very different from the costume originally imagined by McCulley, but very much like the Fairbanks/Power cinematic depictions. Oulie's Zorro was a lone horseman who roamed an imaginary Wild West of fantasy with his horse Toronado as his only friend. Andre Oulie continued to illustrate the adventures of Zorro until 1966, producing nearly 180 installments.

When Andre Oulie retired in 1966, the series was taken over in the paperback monthly magazine, *Zorro,* by Jean Pape, who changed the look of the character to conform more and more to the one that had been created by Disney in the United States. In 1969, the *Zorro Poche* series began a run which would eventually include over 100 issues before being taken up in 1977 by the Italian studio, Del Principe. A few installments of this series were drawn by the illustrator Maxime Roubinet, with covers by Suat

Below, and opposite below: Zorro has been speaking French since 1939. *Opposite page, at top:* A 1986 Zorro comic book, *Zorro in Old California,* featured appearances by Sergeant Garcia and 'Tornado'.

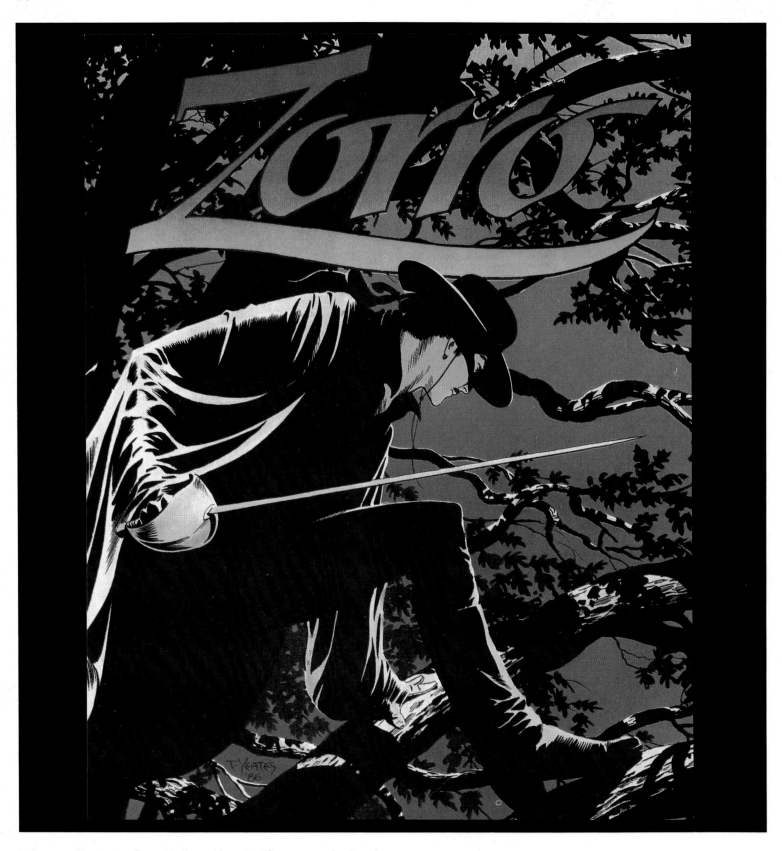

Yalaz, an illustrator from Turkey. Also significant was the handsome book put out in 1978 by Pierre Frisano and Raymond Maric. Abandoned for a dozen years, Zorro then returned in a series of episodes completely illustrated by Robert Rigot, an old hand at French adventure comic strips, who was known for the series *Frederi Le Gardian* that had appeared for many years on the pages of *Coeurs-Vaillants*. A dozen installments were published in 1973 and 1977 which were very similar to the American comic strips based on the 1957-1959 Disney series.

In the Netherlands between 1964 and 1967, another version, illustrated by Hans Kresse, was published in the weekly, *Pep*. Author of the saga of Erik the Viking and of the series of *Peaux-*

Above: The cover of *Zorro in Old California*, by Nedaud and Marcello. Marcello is the creator of The Unknown Horseman and Doctor Justice. *Opposite page:* Alain Delon produced and starred in this 1974 movie as a present to his son.

Rouges (Redskins), Kresse gave a human face to his Zorro which was generally absent in the French version.

In 1985, after the success of the reprise of the Guy Williams series on French television, the comic strip version was taken up by illustrator Arlo Marcello in *Le Journal de Micky*. Creator of a great number of famous heroes, such as The Unknown Horseman and Doctor Justice, Marcello is remembered for giving a modern face to such mythic European heroes as Lancelot, Robin Hood and William Tell.

ZORRO IS BACK!

IT'S ALL FOR FUN AND FUN FOR ALL!

THE ALL NEW Zorro

Emanuel L. Wolf presents **ZORRO** starring **ALAIN DELON** and **STANLEY BAKER**
with **OTTAVIA PICCOLO · MOUSTACHE** and with **ADRIANA ASTI**
Directed by **DUCCIO TESSARI** · Eastmancolor® An Allied Artists Release

PG PARENTAL GUIDANCE SUGGESTED

A New World

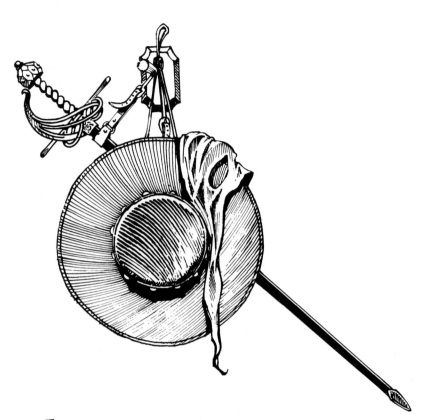

The Renaissance

Guy Williams was a tough act to follow. In the three decades following his television series, the only significant American Zorro films were *The Gay Blade* and a second remake of *The Mark of Zorro* starring Frank Langella in the title role, which was produced for television by Twentieth Century-Fox in 1974. Nearly a decade later, in 1983, the Disney company produced five episodes of a television series in which Henry Darrow became the first Hispanic actor to play Zorro in an American production. The series, called *Zorro and Son*, featured Paul Regina as the masked avenger's scion.

In what was to become another milestone in the history of Zorro's depiction, Gary Goodman and Barry Rosen of New World Television—also known for the highly rated, Emmy Award-nominated series *The Wonder Years* and *Santa Barbara*—undertook in 1989 to produce what was to be the most thoroughly planned and executed Zorro project ever.

Goodman, who entered the film industry in 1972, initially worked with Nicholson-Muir Productions, supervising production for a number of their daytime television shows. He soon began a close association with Howard W. Koch, working on such films as *Plaza Suite* and *The Star Spangled Girl*, before going to Columbia Pictures, where he served as the studio's Director of Development.

Rosen began his film career in New York City, studying film making at the school of visual arts. He won two national awards, the Ford Foundation Award and the Chicago Film Festival Award, and went on to head the in-house production department of Benton & Bowles Advertising, as well as his own production

Above: A scene from the making of the most elaborate production of Zorro to date, New World Television's *Zorro*. Duncan Regehr *(opposite page)* is the latest in the line of illustrious Zorros including Douglas Fairbanks, Tyrone Powers and Guy Williams. Regehr once played Errol Flynn, the original choice for the 1940 Zorro.

company, Vaquer Productions. Having supervised and shot hundreds of commercials all over the world for many major Fortune 500 advertisers, Rosen went on to write, produce and direct several independent features, including *Force Four* and *Devil's Express* for Howard Mahler Films and *Ohio* for Cannon/Universal.

The men formed Goodman-Rosen Productions in 1980, and two years later they produced the independent feature *Longshot*, starring Leif Garret and Linda Manz, before turning their attention to the growing made-for-television film marketplace. In the latter half of the 1980s, they produced a number of highly rated and critically acclaimed movies, beginning with *Quarterback Princess*, the highest rated CBS film in 1983, which starred Helen

At top: John Gertz, son of Mitchell Gertz and president of Zorro Productions, with Bill Dana as Bernardo in *Zorro and Son*. *Below:* Phillip Michael Thomas of Miami Vice appeared in the episode entitled 'Pride of the Pueblo'. *Opposite page:* Regehr as Zorro and Patrice Camhi as Victoria Escalante, Zorro's flame.

ZORRO

Hunt and Don Murray. It was the true story of the first female high school quarterback who *also* became Homecoming Princess. They later produced *Secret Weapons* with Sally Kellerman and Linda Hamilton, a drama about Russian spies. *Going for the Gold: The Bill Johnson Story* was a docudrama about downhill skier Olympic gold medalist Bill Johnson, which starred Anthony Edwards and Dennis Weaver.

For the New World production of *Zorro*, Goodman and Rosen brought Robert McCullough on board as supervising producer. He came to *Zorro* with a wealth of television production experience centered on a writing/producing/directing background that began with NBC-Universal Television's *BJ and the Bear, Sheriff*

Opposite page: Camhi is an award-winning graduate of the Royal Academy of Dramatic Arts, and Regehr *(below and right)* is a classically trained Shakespearean actor who can fill Guy Williams' shoes, cape and hat.

Above: Regehr as Don Diego, and Efram Zimbalist, Jr as Don Alejandro, Zorro's father. Zimbalist was eventually replaced by Henry Darrow in his third Zorro production. Darrow had played an aging Zorro in another generational Zorro story, *Zorro and Son*. as well as being the voice of Zorro in *The New Adventures of Zorro*. *Opposite page* 'Zorro is so much fun to play,' Regehr says. 'It's truly a childhood fantasy come true. Regehr also played swashbuckler Errol Flynn in CBS's *My Wicked Wicked Ways*

Lobo, *Battlestar Gallactica* and *The Six Million Dollar Man* in the 1970s. He had been supervising producer for the first three seasons of *Falcon Crest* and joined Aaron Spelling Productions, where he wrote and produced that season's most highly rated mini-series, *Hollywood Wives*. At Warner Brothers, Bob McCullough was supervising producer of ABC's *Ohara*, an action cop show starring Pat Morita. Immediately before coming to New World for *Zorro*, McCullough was serving at Paramount as supervising producer on *Star Trek: The Next Generation*.

For a story editor, they picked Phillip John Taylor, a graduate of the Royal Academy of Dramatic Art in London who had spent two years as associate director at the American Shakespeare Theater at Stratford, Connecticut. Among Taylor's writing credits were episodes of *All in the Family*, *Mork and Mindy*, *The Incredible Hulk*, *Knightrider* and *The Fall Guy*.

Directors for the New World *Zorro* included many of the finest directors working in television in the late 1980s. Ron Satloff had directed such diverse shows as *Love Boat*, *Perry Mason*, *Hunter* and *Dynasty*. Michael Vejar had directed a number of series, including *Jesse Hawks* starring Robert Conrad, *Magnum PI* with Tom Selleck, *Cagney and Lacey* and *Star Trek: The Next Genera-*

Left: Regehr benefitted from his classical Shakespearean training: like Guy Williams, he learned to fence. *Below*: Regehr, Camhi and Zimbalist all looking somewhat ruffled. *Opposite page*: James Victor portrays Sergeant Mendoza, comic relief in the tradition of Disney's Sergeant Garcia.

Duncan Regehr does his own stunts—including horseback riding—and makes it look easy *above and below*. The actors were trained to ride using Spanish saddles. The horses' tack was specially made by silversmiths and leather craftsmen for authenticity. *At right:* The main cast of characters on location outside Madrid.

tion. Ray Austin entered the film industry as a stuntman and stunt actor and went on to direct such popular television series as *Hawaii 5-0*, *Sword of Justice* and *The Avengers* with Patrick McNee.

Considering the genre, perhaps one of the most important jobs on the production team was that of fight director/stunt coordinator. Peter Diamond was an acknowledged master of screen action, having staged the futuristic laser-light sword fights for all three films of George Lucas' *Star Wars* trilogy. He'd also choreographed the more traditional swashbuckling sword play in Rob Reiner's *The Princess Bride*. Diamond had trained Bob Hoskins for his physically grueling role in *Who Framed Roger Rabbit* and had staged the sword fights in remakes of *The Master of Ballantrae*, *The Man in the Iron Mask*, *Ivanhoe* (with Roger Moore), *The Three Musketeers* and *Treasure Island*. An accomplished fencing master and stunt double, Diamond also had choreographed stage dueling for the Royal London Opera House, The Old Vic, The National Theater and Eight West End Productions in London.

Left: Patrice Camhi's brother—in a guest role—is flanked by Regehr and Victor. *Above:* Regehr, a Canadian, has played an old West character before: Pat Garrett opposite Val Kilmer's Billy the Kid in the Turner Television Network film. Regehr was also a champion figure skater and Olympic boxing contender.

Casting the New World Zorro

Having hand-picked their production team, Gary Goodman and Barry Rosen began to recruit the acting crew that would bring the legend vividly alive in front of the cameras. For Don Alejandro, Zorro's father, they chose Efrem Zimbalist, Jr, best known to television viewers worldwide for his role as FBI Inspector Lew Erskin on the series *The FBI*, which ran on the ABC Network for nine years from 1965 through 1974. Born in New York City, the son of famed violist and composer Efrem Zimbalist

and opera and recording artist Alma Gluck, young Efrem studied acting at the Neighborhood Playhouse, making his Broadway debut in *The Rugged Path*.

Prior to *The FBI*, Zimbalist had starred for six years on the *77 Sunset Strip* series from 1958 until 1964, and his film credits

Opposite page: Efram Zimbalist, Jr's face is familiar to millions of television viewers, due to 16 consecutive years of starring roles on television. *Below:* Regehr with Patrice Camhi and her brother.

Left: Camhi with Zimbalist playing Zorro's father. *Above:* Henry Darrow jumped in the saddle for a third Zorro role. *Below:* Felipe, Zorro's manservant, played by Juan Diego Botta. Fortunately for Botta, Felipe (like Bernardo in the earlier series) is mute. Botta himself doesn't speak a word of English.

included *House of Strangers, By Love Possessed, The Chapman Report, Harlow, Wait Until Dark* and *Airport 1975.* After having spent so many years in contemporary roles, Zimbalist found the role set in nineteenth century California a welcome change. 'Zorro is almost classical in style,' he said. 'This production transposes you into a different mindset with its colorful costumes and sets.' The following year, however, Don Alejandro was recast. The role went to Henry Darrow, who had been the *voice* of Zorro in the 1981 Filmation animated series and who had played Zorro himself in the 1983 *Zorro and Son* series. Darrow thus became the first actor to appear in a leading role in three distinct Zorro productions.

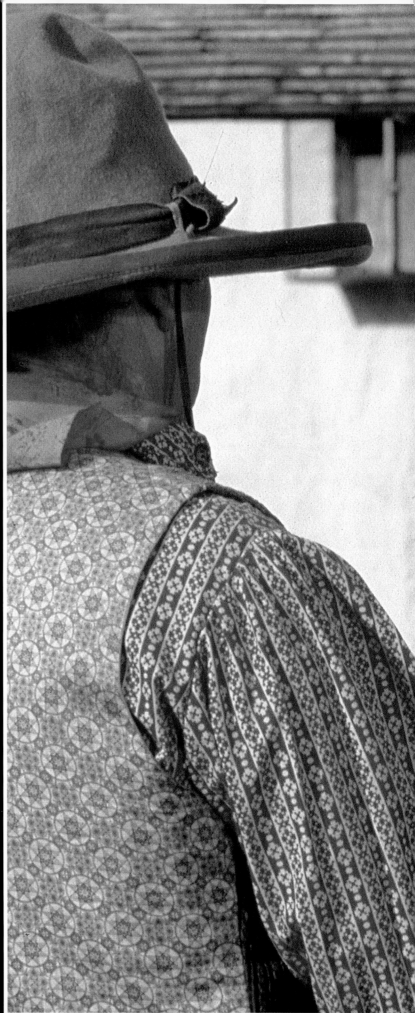

Above, counterclockwise from top left: Zimbalist, Camhi, Tylo, Victor, Regehr and Botta. *Below, left to right, standing:* Tylo, Darrow as the new Alejandro, Regehr and Botta; *(seated)* Victor and Camhi. *Right:* Victor can't get any relief but comic.

The lovely Patrice Camhi, a native of New Mexico, plays Zorro's love interest Victoria Escalante *(opposite)* on New World Television's *Zorro. Above:* Camhi leaves Sergeant Mendoza hanging. *Below:* Señorita and sombrero.

As Victoria Escalante, the romantic interest who would follow in the footsteps of Marguerite de la Motte and Mary Astor, Goodman and Rosen picked young Patrice Camhi, a native New Mexican who had starred opposite Steve Martin and Chevy Chase in the comedy *The Three Amigos*. Camhi also had the distinction of being the only woman to guest star twice as Tom Selleck's love interest in his series *Magnum PI*.

Camhi's interest in acting had begun when she was a teenager. Sam Peckinpah was shooting a film near her hometown and Patrice auditioned as an extra. After she was hired, Peckinpah recognized her talent and gave her a speaking role. She later went on to work with the repertory company La Compania de Teatro de Albuquerque before attending the Royal Academy of Dramatic Arts. Chosen from 3000 aspiring actors, Patrice earned the year's only scholarship to the Royal Academy. Upon completion of the two-and-one-half year program, she received five of the most prestigious awards bestowed by the Academy.

Above: Zorro and Victoria (played by Duncan Regehr and Patrice Camhi), are in love mainly on a plain in Spain. Like Lois Lane, Polly Purebred and other heroes' girlfriends, *Victoria (opposite page) does not know the true identity of Zorro. Zorro has had an* impressive array of girlfriends: Marguerite de la Motte appeared as Lolita in 1920, Mary Astor was Delores in *The Son of Zorro* (1925), and a Sophia Lozarro (who later changed her name to Loren) appeared with Walter Chiari in 1952.

For the role of Sergeant Mendoza—the comic relief buffoon invented by Disney as Sergeant Garcia—Goodman and Rosen chose James Victor, one of the finest character actors on the Hollywood scene. Born in the Dominican Republic, Victor had emigrated with his family to New York City when he was a child, and it was in New York that he was influenced by Miriam Colon's bilingual theater company, where he received his early training.

Victor's work had included the shady lawyer opposite Shelley Long in *Losin' It*. In *Rolling Thunder* he had given William Devane a hard time as Lopez, a barroom brawler, and in the 1989 Oscar-nominated film *Stand and Deliver* he had played an enraged father. On television he had made guest appearances on *Falcon Crest* and *Remington Steele*.

These pages: Three faces of Sergeant Mendoza, played by James Victor. *At top:* Happily feasting. *Above:* Duncan Regehr as Don Diego helps bring the choo-choo to the tunnel. *Right:* Foiled again.

Above: The clutzy Sergeant Mendoza, armed and with an arm already in a sling, draws his weapon, an authentically reproduced flintlock pistol. Unfortunately for the sergeant, these guns were made without safety catches!

Opposite page: Sergeant Mendoza can't seem to get any relief—except comic. True to the time-honored tradition of Noah Beery's Sergeant Gonzales and Henry Calvin's Sergeant Garcia, James Victor plays Sergeant Mendoza as a nincompoon.

Picked as the alcalde (mayor) of Los Angeles, Michael Tylo was a versatile actor who'd had a continuing role on the ABC daytime drama *General Hospital* and had been featured as Dee Boot in the Emmy-nominated 1989 mini-series *Lonesome Dove*. A graduate of Wayne State University with a BFA in acting and an MFA in directing, his extensive theater background included work with the Long Wharf Theater, The Meadowbrook Theater tour, The Alley Theater and a stint at the Kennedy Center in a play under the direction of Richard Chamberlain.

These pages: Michael Tylo plays the Alcalde of Los Angeles whose lawful authority and love of power brings him into conflict with Zorro, a man of the people. The popular support of Zorro further angers the Alcalde, who sees Zorro as a threat to the status quo, and considers Zorro's devotees to be traitors.

Duncan Regehr came to the Zorro role bringing his distinctive style and personality to the classic mold set by such previous Zorros as Douglas Fairbanks, Tyrone Power and Guy Williams. A native of Canada, Regehr had a variety of starring roles in television and films.

'Zorro is so much fun to play,' he laughed. 'It's truly a childhood fantasy come true. An amazing coincidence has happened in that I've had the opportunity to portray *both* Errol Flynn and Zorro, two characters—one real and one fictional—that have defined our image of the swashbuckling hero.'

Ironically, the man picked to play the title role in New World's *Zorro* had actually portrayed Errol Flynn, the man that Twentieth Century-Fox's Darryl F Zanuck had originally wanted to play Zorro in the definitive 1940 big screen version!

In addition to portraying Flynn in the CBS mini-series *My Wicked Wicked Ways*, he brought a mixture of wide classical stage

Opposite page: Zorro is ready to take on all comers with bullwhip, sword and smile. *Above:* The man in black lives by the sword to defend the lady's honor. *Below:* Dunc the hunk as Don Diego.

training, including the contemporary and Shakespearean demands of his period with the renowned Stratford Shakespeare Festival in Ontario, not to mention having been an Olympic boxing contender and champion figure skater.

Regehr also had starred in the CBS series, *Wizards and Warriors,* and in the role of Pat Garrett opposite Val Kilmer's Billy the Kid in the acclaimed Turner Television Network film. His credits also included starring roles in such mini-series as *The Blue and the Grey, The Last Days of Pompeii, Goliath Awaits* and *V.* Among his feature film credits were *Monster Squad* and the title role in Disney's *Earthstar Voyager.*

Before undertaking the role of Zorro, Regehr, who as a classically trained Shakespearean actor was very familiar with fencing, nevertheless had to undergo hours of rigorous training with stunt coordinator and fencing master Peter Diamond in order to approximate the intricate swashbuckling moves for the cameras.

Left: There is no need to ask who this masked man is. *Below:* Alejandro and Victoria are waiting to congratulate a victorious Zorro and Toronado as they raise a little dust and a few hats. *Opposite page:* Hats off to Zorro!

The Production

An international co-production of Zorro Productions, New World Television, The Family Channel in the United States, RAI in Italy and Ellipse Programme/Canal Plus of France, *Zorro* was filmed entirely on location in Spain and at studio facilities just outside of Madrid. Recreating the eighteenth century world of the Spanish dons and señoritas of the rancho society of early California in Spain was a formidable challenge for the producers, cast and crew alike.

Technical accuracy was placed in higher stead than it had ever been in a *Zorro* production. Since California was originally a Spanish colony, researchers from the Spanish National Archives and the California Historical Society provided the production with volumes of material, which included wardrobe sketches, photographs, manuscripts on manners and customs, military uniforms and weapons of the period. Clothing had to be assembled to dress the extras as citizens of the pueblo, and uniforms for a full military garrison had to be created, so costume designers went about producing a full wardrobe for the principal actors, as well as for guest players. Textile merchants and warehouses in

At left: top, center and bottom: The enormous amount of attention, time and money given to the design and construction of the pueblo has resulted in a beautiful and authentic set. *Below:* Great care was given to the clothing and appointments of the principle characters such as Michael Tylo, who plays the Alcalde, as well as the many extras. *Opposite page:* Camhi and her real-life brother, who guest-starred.

Opposite page: The Alcalde wears a beautiful embroidered vest and silk-lined cut-away; the women wear simple cotton dresses. *At top:* Zorro is a two-fisted fighter, as the fearful soldiers flee. *Center and above:* The interior sets were painstakingly created to resemble an actual 1820s hacienda. *At right:* Zorro looks down upon Victoria and Coronado.

Madrid were combed for fabrics that would approximate the look of the period costumes, and silversmiths and leather craftsmen were brought in to recreate costumes actually worn by Spanish noblemen and vaqueros.

For Patrice Camhi, the corsets and layers of embroidered lace undergarments, along with the full dresses, added 25 pounds of weight, which she had to carry gracefully. 'I don't know how women in those days could wear all these clothes, especially in the heat of Los Angeles!' she gasped.

Many of the props and decorative items on the set were faithful reproductions of the original items that Spanish and French craftsmen had made in the early eighteenth century. Certain irreplaceable one-of-a-kind items, such as a diamond bracelet and necklace of the period, gold jewelry made in Mexico City in the 1700s and church-related ornaments were given on loan to the production by various historical societies and museums. These articles were placed under lock and key until they were needed on the set, and an armed guard was posted to look after them.

'In Spain, we were fortunate to have some of the finest and most experienced film technicians and craftsmen,' said supervising producer Bob McCullough. 'The quality and the production values in *Zorro* were on the screen, and certain *not* to go unnoticed!'

Art directors constructed two sets. The first was an elaborate interior set the size of several basketball floors, which were built

Silversmiths and carpenters worked from eighteenth-century originals to reproduce the swords and grates *below*. A team of 125 worked seven weeks to build the sets. *Left:* Don Diego's ruffled blouses are a far cry from the dramatic black worn by Zorro. *Opposite page:* The Alcalde points a stern finger.

Armese contra la gingivitis

El Zorro sabe que Listerine es el **único** enjuage bucal líder sin receta médica aceptado por el Council on Dental Therapeutics de la Asociación Dental Americana, que ataca y ayuda a prevenir a la indeseable placa bacteriana sobre las encías y a la malvada gingivitis, una enfermedad que le da a 3 de cada 4 personas y se caracteriza por la inflamación y a veces hasta el sangrado de las encías. Y como siempre, Listerine mata los gérmenes que causan el mal aliento.

Usted también ¡Ataque a la gingivitis! Visite a su dentista con frecuencia, use cepillo, hilo dental y para mayor protección, use Listerine. El Vencedor.

Su efecto sobre la periodontitis no se ha determinado.

on a sound stage in Madrid. The second was a detailed recreation of the pueblo of Los Angeles, circa 1820, based on the original plans. It was built on a 34-acre lot just 30 miles north of Madrid. For the two sets a team of 50 carpenters, 15 craftsmen, 35 laborers and 25 painters were utilized by the production over a period of seven weeks. This magnificent exterior set, complete with church plaza, military garrison, rancho haciendas, adobe structures, cantina and main street, was designed with several practical interiors to accommodate some interior filming when needed.

So they would feel comfortable and natural on camera wearing eighteenth-century clothing, Regehr and the rest of the cast took to wearing their costumes off-camera prior to the beginning of filming. One night, a cast party was held in a downtown Madrid restaurant and, to the astonishment of the other patrons, all the actors arrived in costume. However, Regehr had discreetly left his Zorro costume at his hotel and came dressed as Don Diego! Too bad!

Especially trained movie horses had to be located and brought to Madrid so they could be readied for their work on *Zorro*. Mules, burros and vehicles of the period, including wagons and buggies, had to be located. The actors were also put through a training period of riding with a Spanish saddle and had to learn how to use weaponry, such as swords and flintlock pistols. Since few Westerns are made today, stunt horses and stuntmen capable of riding and executing various sequences are becoming increasingly rare, but they *were* found.

Opposite page: Zorro gets ready to fight plaque instead of injustice. Guy Williams, Disney's Zorro from 1957-1959, made toothpaste commercials before winning the big role. *Below:* Zorro as he appeared in an advertising campaign for candy in France. *Right:* Duncan Regehr, this generation's Zorro, and Patrice Camhi, as they appear in artwork done by Mario Capaldi for Marvel Comics.

These pages: In the early 1990s, Marvel created a series of Zorro comic books, this time based on the New World television series. Zorro took on the appearance of Guy Williams in the Dell Comic books with the advent of the popular television series shown in 1957; now Marvel has Duncan Regehr, Michael Tylo, Juan Diego Botta and the rest of the New World series' cast as models.

The debut of New World Television's 100-episode *Zorro* on The Family Channel in the United States came in January 1990. Zorro Productions continues to actively develop Zorro for the 1990s and beyond. In December, 1990 Marvel Comics launched its Zorro comic book based upon the New World television series, the most successful launching of a non-superhero comic book in at least five years. The TV series has been so successful that additional episodes are currently being planned. No one yet knows where the series will end, but the current thinking is that there will be at least 100 episodes. Large scale merchandising campaigns are underway in many of the countries in which Zorro is appearing, with hundreds of different toys, books, clothes, and other items that will no doubt become precious to the collectors in the future.

Perhaps most significantly, just as we were going to press with this book, an article appeared on the front page of *The Hollywood Reporter* (April 23, 1991) whose headline read "Spielberg to make sign of the Z for Tri-Star's Zoro." The article quotes Steven Spielberg as saying, "It's a genre of adventure I have loved since I was a kid. I'm looking forward to developing it…"

Why has there been and why is there still so much interest in Zorro?

Zorro has true cross-generational appeal, with four generations of children around the world having grown up with the character. And Zorro has had true staying power because he has so often been successfully reinterpreted within the spirit of the times. Zorro stands out as perhaps the most multi-dimensional character in the pantheon of heroes. He is at once wise, brave, charming, cunning, and very, very romantic.

These pages: The legend of Zorro, born on the pulpy pages of *All Story*, is now available world-wide on VHS and computer disks. The first Zorro floppy-disk computer game, an American innovation, came out in 1985. Filmation released its 1981 Zorro animated series on VHS. Zorro's likeness also appears on a huge assortment of more traditional toys and games, many of which were created in France in 1986 and 1987.

Tyrone
POWER
Linda
DARNELL
in
THE
MARK
OF
Zorro
PRODUCED BY RAYMOND GRIFFITH
DIRECTED BY ROUBEN MAMOULIAN
20th Century-Fox
Encore Triumph

APPENDIX 1
A Comprehensive List
of Johnston McCulley's Zorro Pulp Fiction Stories

Title	Pulp	Volume	Issue	Date
1. The Curse of Capistrano (I)	ALL-STORY WEEKLY	Vol. 100	No. 2	August 9, 1919
2. The Curse of Capistrano (II)	ALL-STORY WEEKLY	Vol. 100	No. 3	August 16, 1919
3. The Curse of Capistrano (III)	ALL-STORY WEEKLY	Vol. 100	No. 4	August 23, 1919
4. The Curse of Capistrano (IV)	ALL-STORY WEEKLY	Vol. 101	No. 1	August 30, 1919
5. The Curse of Capistrano (V)	ALL-STORY WEEKLY	Vol. 101	No. 2	September 6, 1919
6. The Further Adventures of Zorro (I)	ARGOSY	Vol. 142	No. 4	May 6, 1922
7. The Further Adventures of Zorro (II)	ARGOSY	Vol. 142	No. 5	May 13, 1922
8. The Further Adventures of Zorro (III)	ARGOSY	Vol. 142	No. 6	May 20, 1922
9. The Further Adventures of Zorro (IV)	ARGOSY	Vol. 143	No. 1	May 27, 1922
10. The Further Adventures of Zorro (V)	ARGOSY	Vol. 143	No. 2	June 3, 1922
11. The Further Adventures of Zorro (VI)	ARGOSY	Vol. 143	No. 3	June 10, 1922
12. Zorro Rides Again (I)	ARGOSY	Vol. 224	No. 3	October 3, 1931
13. Zorro Rides Again (II)	ARGOSY	Vol. 224	No. 4	October 10, 1931
14. Zorro Rides Again (III)	ARGOSY	Vol. 224	No. 5	October 17, 1931
15. Zorro Rides Again (IV)	ARGOSY	Vol. 224	No. 6	October 24, 1931
16. Zorro Saves A Friend	ARGOSY	Vol. 234	No. 1	November 12, 1932
17. Zorro Hunts A Jackal	ARGOSY	Vol. 237	No. 6	April 22, 1933
18. Zorro Deals With Treason	ARGOSY	Vol. 249	No. 2	August 18, 1934
19. Zorro Hunts By Night	CAVALIER CLASSICS	Vol. 1	No. 2	September 1940
20. The Sign of Zorro (I)	ARGOSY	Vol. 305	No. 2	January 25, 1941
21. The Sign of Zorro (II)	ARGOSY	Vol. 305	No. 3	February 1, 1941
22. The Sign of Zorro (III)	ARGOSY	Vol. 305	No. 4	February 8, 1941
23. The Sign of Zorro (IV)	ARGOSY	Vol. 305	No. 5	February 15, 1941
24. The Sign of Zorro (V)	ARGOSY	Vol. 305	No. 6	February 22, 1941
25. Zorro Draws A Blade	WEST	Vol. 56	No. 2	July 1944
26. Zorro Upsets A Plot	WEST	Vol. 56	No. 3	September 1944
27. Zorro Strikes Again	WEST	Vol. 57	No. 1	November 1944
28. Zorro Saves A Herd	WEST	Vol. 57	No. 2	January 1945
29. Zorro Rides The Gauntlet	WEST	Vol. 57	No. 3	March 1945
30. Zorro Fights A Duel	WEST	Vol. 58	No. 1	May 1945
31. Zorro Opens A Cage	WEST	Vol. 58	No. 2	July 1945
32. Zorro Prevents A War	WEST	Vol. 58	No. 3	September 1945
33. Zorro Fights A Friend	WEST	Vol. 59	No. 1	October 1945
34. Zorro's Hour Of Peril	WEST	Vol. 59	No. 2	November 1945
35. Zorro Slays A Ghost	WEST	Vol. 59	No. 3	December 1945
36. Zorro Frees Some Slaves	WEST	Vol. 60	No. 1	January 1946
37. Zorro's Double Danger	WEST	Vol. 60	No. 2	February 1946
38. Zorro's Masquerade	WEST	Vol. 60	No. 3	March 1946
39. Zorro Stops A Panic	WEST	Vol. 61	No. 1	April 1946
40. Zorro's Twin Perils	WEST	Vol. 61	No. 2	May 1946
41. Zorro Plucks A Pigeon	WEST	Vol. 61	No. 3	June 1946
42. Zorro Rides At Dawn	WEST	Vol. 62	No. 1	July 1946
43. Zorro Takes The Bait	WEST	Vol. 62	No. 2	August 1946
44. Zorro Raids A Caravan	WEST	Vol. 62	No. 3	October 1946
45. Zorro's Moment Of Fear	WEST	Vol. 63	No. 3	January 1947
46. Zorro Saves His Honor	WEST	Vol. 64	No. 1	February 1947
47. Zorro And The Pirate	WEST	Vol. 64	No. 2	March 1947
48. Zorro Beats the Drum	WEST	Vol. 64	No. 3	April 1947
49. Zorro's Strange Duel	WEST	Vol. 65	No. 1	May 1947
50. A Task for Zorro	WEST	Vol. 65	No. 2	June 1947
51. Zorro's Masked Menace	WEST	Vol. 65	No. 3	July 1947
52. Zorro Aids An Invalid	WEST	Vol. 66	No. 1	August 1947
53. Zorro Saves An American	WEST	Vol. 66	No. 2	September 1947
54. Zorro Meets A Rogue	WEST	Vol. 66	No. 3	October 1947
55. Zorro Races With Death	WEST	Vol. 67	No. 1	November 1947
56. Zorro Fights For Peace	WEST	Vol. 67	No. 2	December 1947
57. Zorro Starts The New Year	WEST	Vol. 67	No. 3	January 1948
58. Zorro Serenades A Siren	WEST	Vol. 68	No. 1	February 1948
59. Zorro Meets A Wizard	WEST	Vol. 68	No. 2	March 1948
60. Zorro Fights With Fire	WEST	Vol. 68	No. 3	April 1948
61. Gold For A Tyrant	WEST	Vol. 69	No. 1	May 1948
62. The Hide Hunter	WEST	Vol. 69	No. 2	July 1948
63. Zorro Shears Some Wolves	WEST	Vol. 69	No. 3	September 1948
64. The Face Behind The Mask	WEST	Vol. 70	No. 1	November 1948
65. Hangnoose Reward	WEST	Vol. 70	No. 3	March 1949

Above: 'You wear the Z, señor!' cries Zorro in the story opener of this early Johnston McCulley novelette. When Douglas Fairbanks began the practice of Zorro carving Zs into his opposition, Johnston McCulley appropriated it for his pulp fiction. Later, the mark of Zorro became confined to less vulnerable areas than flesh: the enemy's clothing or a nearby wall.

Tyrone
POWER

Linda
DARNELL

in

THE
MARK
OF
Zorro

PRODUCED BY RAYMOND GRIFFITH
DIRECTED BY ROUBEN MAMOULIAN

20th
Century-Fox   Encore Triumph

These pages: Posters from the classic 1940 Tyrone Power remake (or, 'Encore Triumph') of the original 1920 Douglas Fairbanks movie, also titled *The Mark of Zorro*. This was Tyrone's lone go as the Masked Avenger.

RNELL

THE

ARK

OF

Zorro

PRODUCED BY RAYMOND GRIFFITH
DIRECTED BY ROUBEN MAMOULIAN

20th Century-Fox *Encore Triumph*

APPENDIX 2
Zorro Feature Films

Title	Year	Country	Starring As Zorro	Producer
The Mark of Zorro	1920	USA	Douglas Fairbanks Sr.	Douglas Fairbanks Pictures
Don Q., Son of Zorro	1925	USA	Douglas Fairbanks Sr.	The Elton Corp.
The Bold Caballero	1936	USA	Robert Livingstone	Republic Pictures
The Mark of Zorro	1940	USA	Tyrone Power	20th Century-Fox
Il Sogno di Zorro	1952	Italy	Walter Chiari	??
Zorro the Avenger	1958	USA	Guy Williams	Walt Disney
The Sign of Zorro	1958	USA	Guy Williams	Walt Disney
El Zorro Escarlata	1958	Mexico	??	Importadora, Inc.
El Zorro Vengador	1961	Mexico	Luis Aguilar	??
Zorro Nella Valle dei Fantasmi	1961	Mexico	Jeff Stone	??
Zorro Alla Corte di Spagni	1962	Italy	Giorgio Ardisson	??
La Venganza del Zorro	1962	Spain/Mexico	Frank Latimore	??
Il Segno di Zorro	1962	France/Italy	Sean Flynn	??
L'Ombra di Zorro	1963	Italy/Spain	Frank Latimore	??
La Tre Spade di Zorro	1963	Italy/Spain	Guy Stockwell	??
Zorro E I Tre Moschiettieri	1963	Italy	Gordon Scott	??
Zorro Contro Maciste	1963	Italy	Pierre Brice	??
Il Giuramento di Zorro	1965	Italy/Spain	Tony Russel	??
La Montana Sin Ley	1965	Spain	Jose Suarez	??
Zorro il Ribelle	1966	Italy	Howard Ross	??
I Nippotti di Zorro	1968	Italy	Dean Reed	??
Zorro il Cavaliere della Vendetta	1968	Italy/Spain	Charles Quiney	??
El Zorro la Volpe	1968	Italy	George Ardisson	??
Zorro il Dominatore	1969	Italy/Spain	Charles Quiney	??
El Zorro Justiciero	1969	Italy/Spain	Martin Moore	??
Zorro Alla Corte D'Inghilterra	1969	Italy	Spyros Focas	??
Zorro Marchese di Navarro	1969	Italy	Nadir Moretti	??
Zorro la Maschera della Vendetta	1970	Italy/Spain	Charles Quiney	??
Les Aventures Galantes de Zorro	1972	Belgium	Jean-Michel Dhermay	??
The Erotic Adventures of Zorro	1972	USA	Douglas Frey	RFA
Il Figlio di Zorro	1973	Italy/Spain	Robert Widmark	??
Zorro	1974	Italy/France	Alain Delon	??
El Zorro	1974	Mexico	Julio Aldama	??
Il Sogno di Zorro	1975	Italy	Franco Franchi	??
The Mark of Zorro	1974	USA	Frank Langella	20th Century-Fox
Zorro, the Gay Blade	1980	USA	George Hamilton	Mel Simon Productions

APPENDIX 3
Zorro Republic Serials

Title	Year	Episodes	Starring	Producer
Zorro Rides Again	1937	12	John Carroll	Republic Pictures
Zorro's Fighting Legion	1939	12	Reed Hadley	Republic Pictures
Zorro's Black Whip	1944	12	Linda Sterling	Republic Pictures
Son of Zorro	1947	13	George Turner	Republic Pictures
Ghost of Zorro	1949	12	Clayton Moore	Republic Pictures

APPENDIX 4
Zorro Television Series

Title	Year Began	Episodes	Starring As Zorro	Producer
Zorro	1957	78	Guy Williams	Walt Disney Productions
The New Adventures of Zorro	1981	13	Animated Series	Filmation Productions
Zorro and Son	1983	6	Henry Darrow	Walt Disney Productions
Zorro	1989	75 (+ ?)	Duncan Regehr	New World

Posters from *Ghost of Zorro* (*above*) and the *Son of Zorro* serial (*below*), both produced by Republic Pictures. Moore, a former circus aerialist and male model, got his start in movies as a stunt-man.

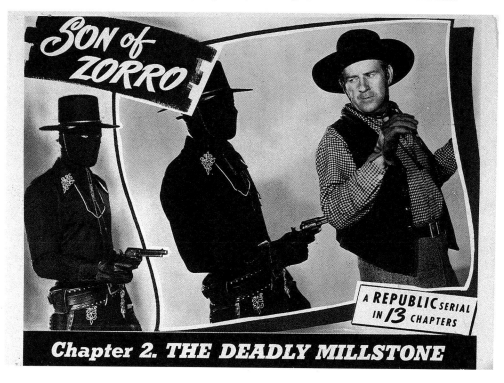

Just a few of the many Zorro-inspired products designed post-Disney and before the success of the New World Television series. *This page, clockwise from the action figures:* American action figures (1982), a French bath towel (1986), a French puppet (1986), a French teepee (1987), a European costume (1989) and French masks (1986). *In the center:* Mug, candy, belt, bathing suit, baby outfit and briefcase.

This page, clockwise from the clock: An English clock (1989), French poster (1986), a French riding toy and ball (both 1986), French glassware and boots (both 1987). *In the center:* Sweatsuits, socks, holster and gun.

Disney Era Collectible Zorro Merchandise

I. Toys and Antique Collectibles

	Item	Manufacturer	Value Today
1.	3-D cut out, plastic dress up kit	Aldon	$ 100.00
2.	7-UP pins	7-UP Company	$ 25.00
3.	Action set with 2 chalk-tipped swords, hat and mask	Marx	$ 350.00
4.	Activity box	Whitman	$ 100.00
5.	Arcade card(s)??	??	$ 20.00
6.	Bean bag target game	Gardner Toys	$ 150.00
7.	Belt buckle, metal	??	$ 75.00
8.	Black shirt	??	$ 100.00
9.	Board game, 1965	Parker Brothers	$ 150.00
10.	Board game, 1958	Whitman	$ 175.00
11.	Board game, 1965	Whitman	$ 75.00
12.	Boot mug, blue plastic, with 'Z' handle	??	$ 30.00
13.	Candy tin, cylindrical	Sorfim	$ 100.00
14.	Cap pistol	Marx	$ 100.00
15.	Charm bracelet, brass	??	$ 100.00
16.	Color-by-number set with colored pencils	Transogram	$ 100.00
17.	Color-by-numbers set	Hassenfeld	$ 75.00
18.	Coloring book, 1958	Whitman	$ 30.00
19.	Costume and mask	Ben Cooper	$ 75.00
20.	Costume and mask (based on Filmation series)	Ben Cooper	$ 35.00
21.	Hat and mask, felt	Benay Albee	$ 10.00
22.	Costume and mask, Deluxe model	Ben Cooper	$ 125.00
23.	Cuff links and tie clasp	??	$ 50.00
24.	Dish set, ceramic, with cup, plate and bowl	??	$ 100.00
25.	Domino set	Halsam	$ 75.00
26.	Dry cleaning bag costume, paper	Emery	$ 75.00
27.	Erasable coloring slates	Transogram	$ 50.00
28.	Figure on horse, 12' plastic	Marx	$ 125.00
29.	Figure, blue ceramic	??	$ 200.00
30.	Figures, 2.5 inches, Zorro with Toronado	Lido	$ 50.00
31.	Figures, 4 inches, Zorro with Toronado	Lido	$ 50.00
32.	Figures, 7 inches, Zorro with Toronado	Lido	$ 50.00
33.	Film strips with viewer	Lido	$ 50.00
34.	Flashlight flip top hat and mask, yellow plastic	Bantamlite	$ 75.00
35.	Flintlock pistol with hat and mask	Marx	$ 150.00
36.	Flintlock rifle	Marx	$ 250.00
37.	Gloves	Wells Lamont	$ 40.00
38.	Gum stickers (??)	Super Novelty Candy Co.	$ 10.00 apiece
39.	Gym bag, red ??	??	$ 100.00
40.	Handpuppet	Gund	$ 100.00
41.	Hat and mask	Bailey	$ 15.00
42.	Hat and mask, plastic	Benay Albee	$ 20.00
43.	Holster set with belt, holster, and pistol	Marx	$ 200.00
44.	Jigsaw puzzle with frame, 'Flashing Steel'	Jaymar	$ 33.00
45.	Jigsaw puzzle with frame, 'Sgt. Garcia & Diego'	Jaymar	$ 33.00
46.	Jigsaw puzzle with frame, 'The Avenger'	Jaymar	$ 33.00
47.	Jigsaw puzzle with frame, 'The Duel'	Jaymar	$ 33.00
48.	Jigsaw puzzle with frame 1965	Whitman	$ 30.00
49.	Lunchbox with thermos, red and black, 1957	Alladin	$ 40.00
50.	Lunchbox with thermos, red and black, 1965	Alladin	$ 40.00
51.	Magic writing slate - complex model	Strathmore	$ 60.00
52.	Magic writing slate - simple model	Strathmore	$ 30.00
53.	Model kit	Aurora	$ 200.00
54.	Paint By Numbers set	Hasbro	$ 85.00
55.	Pen flashlight	Bantamlight	$ 50.00
56.	Pencil sharpener	??	$ 60.00
57.	PEZ dispenser, 3 versions	PEZ	$ 50.00 each
58.	Pinwheel	??	$ 25.00
59.	Playset with fort, cannons, soldiers, cave, Zorro	Marx	$2500.00
60.	Polo shirt with mask and cardboard stand-up	??	$ 45.00
61.	Postcard fan with Don Diego (2 versions)	Disney	$ 10.00
62.	Ring, plastic with black stone (??)	??	$ 15.00
63.	Rub-ons	Hasbro	$ 50.00
64.	Rug	??	$ 150.00

I. Toys and Antique Collectibles

	Item	Manufacturer	Value Today
65.	School bag with shoulder strap	??	$ 100.00
66.	School tablets, 4 different, with cut-out mask	Westab	$ 25.00 each
67.	Secret Sight scarf mask	Westminster Mfg.	$ 40.00
68.	String bolo ties (2 versions)	??	$ 100.00 each
69.	Sun pictures	??	$ 30.00
70.	Sunglasses	??	$ 40.00
71.	Super-8 mm. film of 'Zorro Rides Again'	United Artists	$ 100.00
72.	Sword, rubber and plastic	Marx	$ 20.00
73.	T-shirt, black, with 'Disney's Zorro'	Fruit of the Loom	$ 50.00
74.	T-shirt, white, with 'Disney's Zorro'	Shintees	$ 40.00
75.	Target board with dart shooting rifle	R.T. Cohn, Inc.	$ 200.00
76.	Target game and pistol	Knickerbocker Plastic Co.	$ 250.00
77.	Target set with 2 guns, 4 darts, and target	Lido	$ 75.00
78.	Topps cards (set of 88)	Topps	$ 200.00
79.	Topps cards, box only	Topps	$ 200.00 each
80.	Topps cards, wrappers only	Topps	$ 100.00 each
81.	True-vue card in sleeve	Viewmaster	$ 75.00
82.	U.S. Time watch	Ingersol/Timex	$ 150.00
83.	Viewmaster (3 reels)	Viewmaster	$ 75.00
84.	Wallet	??	$ 100.00
85.	Wallet - 1966	??	$ 50.00
86.	Water pistol	Knickerbocker	$ 75.00
87.	Whip set with whip, mask, ring, lariat, pistol, 2 fencing foils, and knife	Shimmel	$ 125.00
88.	Wrist flashlight, 3 color	Bantamlite	$ 75.00

II. Records

	Item	Manufacturer	Value Today
1.	Record, 12", '4 Adventures of Zorro' with Guy Williams	Disneyland Records	$ 50.00
2.	Record, 12", 'Songs About Zorro & Other Heroes'	Mickey Mouse Club Records	$ 50.00
3.	Record, 7", Mitch Miller & the Sandpipers 'Zorro' with 6 color sleeve and orange vinyl, b/w ?	Golden Records	$ 75.00
4.	Record, 7", The Chordettes 'Zorro' with cream and red sleeve, b/w 'Love is a 2-Way Street'	Cadence Records	$ 50.00
5.	Record, 7", The Chordettes 'Zorro' with cream and red sleeve, b/w 'Lollipop'	Barnaby Records	$ 50.00

III. Comics

1.	Dell 882 (Toth)	Dell
2.	Dell 920 (Toth)	Dell
3.	Dell 933 (Toth)	Dell
4.	Dell 960 (Toth)	Dell
5.	Dell 976 (Toth)	Dell
6.	Dell 1003	Dell
7.	Dell 1037	Dell
8.	Sep-Nov #7	Gold Key?
9.	Dec-Feb #8	Gold Key?
10.	Dec-Feb #920 (?)	Gold Key?
11.	Mar-May #9	Gold Key?
12.	Jun-Aug #10	Gold Key?
13.	Sep-Nov #11	Gold Key?
14.	Topps (1961?) 'Runaway Witness'	Topps
15.	Golden Keys issues 1-9, republished 1965	Golden Keys

Left: The cast of the New World Zorro on the set near Madrid in 1991. *Above:* Duncan Regehr on the most recent mount to play the heroic role as Zorro's always loyal Toronado.

APPENDIX 6
Zorro: List of Disney Episodes
(Total Episodes: 78)

1. PRESENTING SEÑOR ZORRO
2. ZORRO'S SECRET PASSAGE
3. ZORRO RIDES TO THE MISSION
4. THE GHOST OF THE EAGLE
5. ZORRO'S ROMANCE
6. ZORRO SAVES A FRIEND
7. ZORRO SETS A TRAP
8. ZORRO RIDES INTO TERROR
9. A FAIR TRIAL
10. GARCIA'S SWEET MISSION
11. DOUBLE TROUBLE FOR ZORRO
12. THE LUCKIEST SWORDSMAN ALIVE
13. THE FALL OF MONTASERIO
14. SHADOW OF DOUBT
15. GARCIA STANDS ACCUSED
16. SLAVES OF THE EAGLE
17. SWEET FACE OF DANGER
18. ZORRO FIGHTS HIS FATHER
19. DEATH STACKS THE DECK
20. AGENT OF THE EAGLE
21. ZORRO SPRINGS A TRAP
22. THE UNMASKING OF ZORRO
23. THE SECRET OF THE SIERRA
24. THE NEW COMMANDMENTS
25. THE FOX AND THE COYOTE
26. ADIÓS SEÑOR ZORRO
27. THE EAGLES BROOD
28. ZORRO BY PROXY
29. QUINTANA MAKES A CHOICE
30. CONSPIRACY
31. THE MAN WITH THE WHIP
32. THE CROSS OF THE ANDES
33. THE MISSING JEWELS
34. THE WELL OF DEATH
35. THE TIGHTENING NOOSE
36. THE SERGEANT REGRETS
37. THE EAGLE LEAVES THE NEST
38. BERNARDO FACES DEATH
39. DAY OF DECISION
40. WELCOME TO MONTEREY
41. ZORRO RIDES ALONE
42. HORSE OF ANOTHER COLOR
43. THE SEÑORITA MAKES A CHOICE
44. RENDEZVOUS AT SUNDOWN
45. THE NEW ORDER
46. AN EYE FOR AN EYE
47. THE FLAG OF TRUCE
48. AMBUSH
49. PRACTICAL JOKER
50. THE FLAMING ARROW
51. THE RUNAWAYS
52. THE IRON BOX
53. ZORRO FIGHTS A DUEL
54. AMNESTY FOR ZORRO
55. THE GAY CABALLERO
56. TORNADO IS MISSING
57. ZORRO VERSUS CUPID
58. THE LEGEND OF ZORRO
59. SPARK OF REVENGE
60. THE MISSING FATHER
61. PLEASE BELIEVE ME
62. THE BROOCH
63. THE MOUNTAIN MAN
64. THE HOUND OF THE SIERRA
65. MANHUNT
66. THE MAN FROM SPAIN
67. TREASURE FOR THE KING
68. EXPOSING THE TYRANT
69. ZORRO TAKES A DARE
70. AN AFFAIR OF HONOR
71. THE SERGEANT SEES RED
72. INVITATION TO DEATH
73. THE CAPTAIN REGRETS
74. MASQUERADE FOR MURDER
75. LONG LIVE THE GOVERNOR
76. THE FORTUNE TELLER
77. SEÑOR CHINA BOY
78. FINDERS KEEPERS

APPENDIX 7
Zorro: New World TV Episodes
First Season

1-4. 'The Legend Begins' (Parts I-IV)
   -written by Robert McCullough
5. 'Dead Men Tell No Tales'
   -written by Philip John Taylor
6. 'Whereabouts'
   -written by Jim Wells
7. 'The Bounty Hunters'
   -written by John Philip Taylor
8. 'The Best Man'
   -written by Robert L. McCullough
9. 'All That Glitters'
   -written by Richard Freiman
10. 'Honor Thy Father'
   -written by Adam Tyler
11. 'A Wolf in Sheeps Clothing'
   -written by Paul and Sharon Boorstin

12. 'The Deceptive Heart'
   -by Bruce Lansbury
13. 'Water'
   -written by Ron Friedman
14. 'The Magician'
   -written by Ted Alben and Greg Klein
15. 'Zorro's 'Other Woman'
   -written by Greg O'Neill
16. 'Deal with the Devil'
   -written by Suzanne Herrera
17. 'Double Entendre'
   -written by Robert L. McCullough
18. 'Ghost Story'
   -witten by Paul and Sharon Boorstin
19. 'An Explosive Situation'
   -written by Philip John Taylor

20. 'The Unhappy Medium'
   -written by Bruce Lansbury
21. 'Palomarez Returns'
   -written by Robert L. McCullough
22. 'The Sure Thing'
   -written by Robert L. McCullough
23. 'Pride of the Pueblo'
   -written by Ted Alben and Greg Klein
24. 'Child's Play'
   -written by Marta Victoria
25. 'Family Business'
   -written by Philip John Taylor

APPENDIX 8
Zorro: New World TV Episodes
Second Season

26. 'The White Sheep of the Family'
    -written by Philip John Taylor
27. 'He Who Lives by the Sword...'
    -written by Philip John Taylor
28. 'The Chase'
    -written by Michael Marks
29. 'Freedom Of The Press'
    -written by Bruce Lansbury
30. 'The Devil's Fortress' Part 1
    -written by Philip John Taylor
31. 'The Devil's Fortress' Part 2
    -written by Philip John Taylor
32. 'The Challenge'
    -written by Robert L. McCullough
33. 'The Wizard'
    -written by Robert L. McCullough
34. 'One Special Night'
    -written by Gary Stephen Rieck

35. 'The Don's Dilemma'
    -written by Adam Tyler
36. 'The Marked Man'
    -written by Greg O'Neill
37. 'Master and Pupil'
    -written by Robert L. McCullough
38. 'The Tease'
    -written by Robert L. McCullough
39. 'Broken Heart, Broken Mask'
    -written by Eugene Pressman
40. 'The Falcon'
    -written by Andrew Burg and Scott Myers
41. 'The Old Flame'
    -written by Tom Sawyer
42. 'Sanctuary'
    -written by Tim Minear
43. 'Kidnapped'
    -written by Philip John Taylor

44. 'Big Brother'
    -written by Philip John Taylor
45. 'The Whistling Bandit'
    -written by Tim Minear
46. 'To Be a Man'
    -written by Bruce Lansbury
47. 'Alejandro Rides Again'
    -written by Richard Freiman
48. 'It's A Wonderful Zorro'
    -written by Philip John Taylor
49. 'The Newcomers'
    -written by Robert L. McCullough
50. 'Rites of Passage'
    -written by Robert L. McCullough

APPENDIX 9
Zorro: New World TV Episodes
Third Season

51. 'The Three Musketeers' Part 1
    -written by Philip John Taylor
52. 'The Three Musketeers' Part 2
    -written by Philip John Taylor
53. 'The Jeweled Sword'
    -written by Bruce Lansbury
54. 'Heir Apparent'
    -written by Robert L. McCullough
55. 'Armed and Dangerous'
    -written by Robert L. McCullough
56. 'A New Broom'
    -written by Philip John Taylor
57. 'The Buccaneers' Part 1
    -written by Robert L. McCullough
58. 'The Buccaneers" Part 2
    -written by Robert L. McCullough
59. 'A New Lease On Love'
    -written by Philip John Taylor

60. 'Turning The Tables'
    -written by Tim Minear
61. 'A Love Remembered'
    -written by Joe Gunn
62. 'Mendoza The Malevolent'
    -written by Robert L. McCullough
63. 'Wicked, Wicked Zorro'
    -written by Robert L. McCullough
64. 'Rush to Judgment'
    -written by Philip John Taylor
65. 'Test of Faith'
    -written by Robert L. McCullough
66. 'Dirty Tricks'
    -written by Philip John Taylor
67. 'Silk Purses and Sows Ears'
    -written by Robert L. McCullough
68. 'Miracle of the Pueblo'
    -written by Philip John Taylor

69. 'A Woman Scorned'
    -written by Philip John Taylor
70. 'They Call Her Annie'
    -written by Robert L. McCullough
71. 'The Word'
    -written by Robert L. McCullough
72. 'The Man Who Cried Wolf'
    -written by Bruce Lansbury
73. 'Balancing the Books'
    -written by Robert L. McCullough
74. 'Blind Man's Bluff'
    -written by Philip John Taylor
75. 'Every Man A Hero'
    -written by Robert L. McCullough

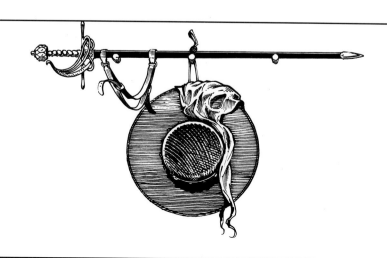

INDEX